A Boy Growing Up During The Great Depression

What Life Was Like in America in the 1930s

By Just Hallen

+ Grove School 1931 Northbrook, Illinois

Glenbrook Gardens Peony Show Garden

Our Home, 1935

Early picture Grove School, about 1865

My Dad Ray B. Hallen

Preface

On December 18th, 1974 I received a call from the president of my advertising agency's largest client. He informed me they would no longer be our client. That call was the beginning of the end of the ad agency I had started 25 years earlier in a small one-room office with no windows and no clients.

With the loss of this client I decided to sell the ad agency that had serviced National and International Corporations from offices in Chicago, Los Angeles and Salt Lake City. What had started very small had been quite successful and I often wondered, "Why was I so lucky?"

I was self educated with little formal schooling. When I did attend Monmouth and St. Mary's Colleges briefly I skipped most classes and spent my time reading and teaching myself Latin and Medieval History.

I learned print advertising art and design by working at commercial art studios in Chicago. I trained as a copywriter by writing commercials for an Iowa television station.

I started the business in 1960 when it was the belief that Fifty Thousand Dollars minimum was needed to start an advertising agency in the United States. I had no money and was earning very little from a job selling background music. I was 38 years old and time was against me. I opened the business anyway and began looking for clients.

This was all because of a decision I made at the age of 12. By then I had already made the major determination that would affect my entire life. I had decided to own and operate my own business. I was slowed down briefly by financial conditions but self employment was the driving force in my life and forever my principal objective. Matter of fact, at 12 I was already a self employed commission catalog salesman for Montgomery Ward.

People often ask me what life was like in America when I was 12 years old? The country was in the middle of The Great Depression. Opportunities seemed very limited. I should have been discouraged. I was never discouraged because the reality was that it was my very good fortune to grow up during the 1930s. It was my privilege to live during those "Hard Times" years.

I thought it would be an inspiration to people today to know what we went through and to understand what it was like to live when money was scarce and jobs nonexistent much of the time. That is the reason for this book.

I want to give a true account of a boy's life growing up during the Great Depression and to paint an accurate picture of how real people were living during the 1930s. I tell exactly what our lives were really like day by day when radio was the primary source of family entertainment. There was no television, video games, cell phones or computers, no

mother and father. The only part of the movie I remember distinctly was something that confused me. It was a scene where a man in shirt sleeves dipped his whole arm into a bath tub full of water. When I saw him do the same thing a second time I was really puzzled. It was about then that my dad said something to my mother and we left the theater. That must have been the point at which we had come in to the movie. In those days movies were made in such a way that it didn't matter if a person came in at the beginning of the show or not. Once seated everyone would catch on to the plot very quickly. We went to that same Barrington movie house, named the Catlow, several times and I was always attracted to the bright colored lights around the ticket office. I don't know why I remember the name of the theater, but don't remember being inside, except the time I saw the man and the bathtub.

There was a small cinder driveway from the road to the gate and apartment. Someone took a picture of my uncle John and a couple more people in front of the gate and when I saw the photograph many years later it looked so familiar I felt I must have been there when it was taken. I have a picture of myself standing behind a Dodge car that was also taken in that driveway. These pictures and the Catlow movie house make up the extent of the memories of my very early life in Barrington.

II

We lived in Barrington until 1924, when my father took a job as General Manager of Northbrook Gardens, a peony farm and nursery. I spent the most important four years of my formative life on that peony farm. The property was located on Dundee Road, about two and a half miles northwest of the center of the Village of Northbrook, a small town of less than a thousand souls. Northbrook is about 20 miles directly north of downtown Chicago.

At Northbrook Gardens we lived in a pleasant two story white frame house. I remember the house, yard and peony fields clearly. The front porch, with its colonial style columns, ran from one end of the house to the other. The big front door in the middle of the house opened into the living room. We rarely used the front door, but went in and out through the kitchen door, located at the rear of the house. The driveway and the peony farm itself were east and north of our home.

The front yard lawn started as a slight hill that ran down from the front porch to a white wooden fence that was parallel with Dundee Road. There were two very tall spruce trees in the middle of the lawn. At the west end of the front yard was a big Snow Apple tree that produced what I thought to be some of the most delicious apples in the world. Snow Apples were about average size, bright red, with snow white flesh, from which came the name. I have never seen Snow Apples any other place in the country.

The kitchen, which was not very big, had a huge cast iron coal stove with removable covers over the scorching heat. Covers could be removed, even when hot, with a handle that fit into a slot in the cover. There was also a tank in the stove that contained hot water. A big black pipe ran up through the roof. In winter it was always cozy and warm in the kitchen. I remember it so well because we used the kitchen more than any other room, just like most rural families did when ice cold wind was blowing the snow in drifts outside.

We ate almost all our meals in the kitchen. Being from Sweden my parents were used to eating quite a bit of fish. There was a Swedish fish man who came around regularly and herring with a lot of peeled boiled potatoes was often our main meal. I did not like herring because it had so many bones. I also disliked the long woolen stockings I had to wear in very cold weather. They made my legs itch uncomfortably.

Bedrooms were all upstairs, as well as the single bathroom. My brothers Elmer and Paul where born while we lived in that house. Until they arrived on the scene I had a bedroom all to myself. I must have been comfortable there because one night, during one of the frequent summer thunderstorms, my mother, who was worried about me, said she came in and found me sound asleep despite the lightning and thunder.

Some time during my 4th year I contracted Diphtheria, a deadly illness at the time, and almost died. Medical facilities were not the best in Northbrook. If a local doctor named

Larsen treated me my survival must have been somewhat miraculous.

In back of our house was a large grass yard and behind that a two story white building that served as a garage and work area for dividing and shipping peony roots. It was distinguishable by a long slopping roof. Behind that building was a short narrow cinder lane and the small home of our nearest neighbor. I don't remember the people who lived in the house, but their yard was a mess of old junk.

A few yards east of our home stood a small frame building that was supposed to be my father's office, although he never used it except for some storage. It was a good place for me to hide out once in awhile. Once when about four, a picture of me and my dad was taken by my mother. I was standing along side the office, next to a wheel barrow that dad held up by its handles. I remembered the day that picture was taken when I saw it again many years later

The land east of the "office" and along the main highway, Dundee Road, was the actual farm itself. There were more than 10 acres of many rows of peony plants and a show garden for exhibiting the several varieties of peonies. There was a pond near the middle of the rows of peonies..

The owner of Northbrook Gardens was a man named Paul Batty. The Batty family lived in Glencoe on the shore of Lake Michigan, a few miles east of Northbrook Gardens. They had a daughter, quite a bit older than me, named Ruby. I remember visiting their home several times. Once when Ruby had a bad cough her mother referred to it by saying "Ruby is barking".

Adjoining the east side of the peony field was Sky Harbor Airport, with the north-south runway very close to our fence. When we moved to the property the airport was still under construction. It was built to accommodate wealthy airplane owners, mostly residents of Lake Michigan's North Shore. The airport had a short period of prosperity although it was in operation until well after the Depression was over. Sky Harbor opened for business in June 1929 but was doomed by the '29 Crash. The art deco terminal building had a fine restaurant called The Petrushka and a good size auditorium with a fully equipped stage. Many professional night club acts performed there before the Great Depression. After the Stock Market crash the acts during the 30s were mostly amateur theatricals. In the late 1930s, during the worst of the depression, the terminal was closed, and after being ransacked by vandals was demolished. The building would have been an historical treasure had it survived.

I think the reason I remember so much about Northbrook Gardens is because when my dad left to establish his own peony farm, the new manager of Northbrook Gardens and his family soon became friends with our family. The Christmans were from Minneapolis and had a son, Billy, who was slightly younger than me. Billy quickly became my best friend. So I spent as much time back at the old place as Billy did at my new home. When I obtained a hand cranked movie projector Billy and I spent many hours looking at old black and white movies in a dark cold storage room at Billy's. We decided we would make movies ourselves some day, and named our company H&C Movie Company. Billy was 9 and I was 11. Unfortunately Billy was killed in a car crash at 17 years of age. I was shocked and his parents, who were slightly older than my own mom and dad, never fully recovered from Billy's death, Both parents died a few years after Billy. Although the families ran competitive peony farms only a half mile apart, each had their own customers and there was never any personal relationship other than family friendship. I remember the Christmans with great affection and recall being in their home many happy hours.

III

In 1924 when we came to the town of Northbrook the streets in the business center were still mostly unpaved mud and people walked on wooden sidewalks. It was typical rural America, although only 20 miles north of Chicago, then America's second largest city. But those 20 miles separated an entire generation in way of life. Northbrook was a hick town, while Chicago was sophistication itself (or so the Chicago residents thought).

When it rained, the streets in Northbrook became almost impassable. Mud holes, ruts and deep pools of water challenged even the rugged Model T Ford and the most skillful driver. The Model T was the most popular car in town, as it was in most of the country at the time, and for many years to come. My dad had a black 1924 Model T four door sedan.

Henry Ford was famous for telling customers they could have a Model T in any color, as long as it was black. Old Henry became my idol when I learned how he had built the Ford Motor Company and changed the whole country.

The Milwaukee Railroad tracks ran north and south, right through the center of town. When my Grandfather Morfar (Mother's Father in Swedish) came from Chicago during an exceptionally rainy day he would have to get off the train in Techny. That was the station one stop before, and about 2 miles south, of Northbrook. The Techny station had a brick area around it for easier access in the rain. The name came from its original location as St. Joseph's Technical School, later shortened to Techny. The school operated for 12 years, instructing boys in various trades. Then in 1909 a training center for missionary priests and brothers opened at the location. The student priests also worked at a nursery the school owned and operated. My dad often bought evergreens and other plants he used in his business from the Techny nursery. Some times I would accompany him and thought it strange to see the young priests working in the nursery fields clad in their long black frocks.

My mother's parents had come from Sweden, bringing mom when she was nine years old. My grandfather Morfar had been raised in Germany but moved to Sweden and became a Swedish citizen in order to emigrate to the United States under the Swedish quota. Quotas for Germans were used more rapidly while Sweden rarely used all of theirs. Morfar was a jeweler by trade and became a diamond importer in the United

States. We kids called grandfather Muffa. My grandmother, Mormor, had operated a pool hall and tavern in Malmo, Sweden before her marriage. My dad's father was in the Swedish Military and a guard to Swedish Kings Oscar II and Gustaf V. Dad's father's name was Emil Gustafson, but the last name was changed to Hallen upon his retirement. Name change was the custom for military retirees in Sweden. Hallen came from Hallenberg, the name of the town where he lived. Neither of my father's parents ever came to America. Of their six children only my dad and two brothers, Terry and Ivar, ever came and lived in the United States. As a result my brothers and I had few cousins in this country. Most of dad's family remained and presently live in Sweden. One uncle in Stockholm I remember talking with on the telephone was named Sexton. He was a school teacher and spoke English with a decided British accent.

By age five I clearly remember a great deal about my life, even before I started school. One time I was running as fast as I could through our backyard, just at dusk, when I was caught under the chin by my mother's clothes line. The line flipped me up in the air and I landed on my back with a crash. I also recall telling fantastic stories to the workers on the peony farm, as well as other children in the neighborhood. They were tales of an imaginary older brother and of the wild animals my "brother" and I owned. I suspect they didn't believe me because my stories were too fantastic to be even reasonable. What stimulated my imagination is still a mystery. My real brother Elmer was born in June, 1924. Many of the workers on the peony farm were immigrants from Germany and Sweden. I could speak Swedish fairly well for a kid and was often the translator between the Swedes and the foreman on the job. I also learned quite a bit of German by listening to the men, but one of the new Germans spoke English as well, so I wasn't needed as much with them. But most of all, I remember in particular that one afternoon during my 5th year we had a violet thunderstorm. The kids at Grove School, which was about a half mile west of where we lived, told me in graphic detail about the thunder, lightening and fierce wind during the storm.

In 1927, at 6 years of age, I started the first grade in Grove School, a one room wooden building, typical of rural America. Grove School got its name because of its location in a large grove of oak and hickory trees. Similar groves are found throughout the flat prairie land of Northern Illinois. The area was known as Hickory Grove. The school address was simply Dundee Road, the highway that connected the towns of Dundee, 30 miles west, and Glencoe, 10 miles east. Dundee Road was one of the first concrete paved highways in Illinois.

Grove School had been built in 1858 and used continuously since then, even during the Civil War. I never heard anyone talk about the school's long history, although generations of nearby farmers had attended classes there.

My teacher's name was Miss Rachel. We kids didn't use the last names of teachers in those days. I remember her only as coaching me as an Indian Brave in the school play

"Hiawatha". We had so many rehearsals I soon memorized every kid's part.

The vacant land adjacent to the west side of the school property, in the same grove of trees, was where my father's own peony garden would be located in the future and where we would live. I don't know if he had bought the property yet. I had been very anxious to start school ever since I first watched the older boys and girls coming home when I was still 5 years old. I was envious of them but couldn't even begin to imagine what school life was really like. One night before I was old enough for school we had another violent thunderstorm. My dad was away and during the lightening, thunder and wind, a huge tree crashed into our dining room, destroying a big window and the dining room table. That experience, and other storms, caused me much distress for the next few years.

During the 1920s there was a period of very violent weather. It seemed to me the weather became much milder during the Dust Bowl Days of the thirties. By the time I was in high school in 1939 we didn't have those storms very often. At least I don't remember any of them. This violet weather made me afraid of thunderstorms, or even the threat of a storm. Although there was no system for warning of tornados in the 20s, there were graphic pictures in the newspapers of funnel cloud damage. So during my first year at Grove School I tried every possible excuse to stay home if the weather looked threatening. I guess because of my experiences with thunder storms I became very frightened when it looked as though we would have another outbreak of violent weather, possibly with damaging winds. Unfortunately for me I never could come up with a convincing reason why I should stay home. My fake claim that I had to go to the bathroom too frequently to attend school never worked either.

In class I remember looking out the window at the skies over the old cemetery west of the school and speculating as to whether they were getting darker and more threatening or not. When the dark clouds looked particularly ominous some parents would come to school and pick up their kids. My parents did not. Although I suppose my mother reassured me, I had no way of knowing if she knew what she was talking about either. I realized as an adult with children of my own that my parents were not aware of the psychological effect my previous experience with thunderstorms had on me. My dad used to ridicule my fear by imitating my down turned mouth when I was afraid of the unknown. I never felt anger at him because, like most young parents, my father was inexperienced and didn't understand my fear. Perhaps, subconsciously, this fear of bad weather was one reason I became interested in meteorology in later life, and even briefly did some weather forecasting for a company that specialized in long range weather trends for agricultural businesses. My brother Paul was born in August, 1927 at Northbrook Gardens

There were humorous happenings in my life then too. Once when I found a package of my dad's cigarettes some place. I opened the pack and although didn't attempt to smoke any, I couldn't put them back in such a way that their being opened wouldn't be noticed. So I simply threw away the one I taken out of the pack and substituted a new cigarette I made out of something, I don't remember what I could have used. It looked pretty good to me, but I was worried never the less. But, rather than punishing me, my father was so amused at my pathetic "cigarette" he just told me not to worry about it, and not to do it again. I never became a smoker, but I don't think it was because of this incident.

IV

A very popular pass time during the 1920s and 30s was reading the comic strips in the newspapers. The "funnies" were America's major source of entertainment before radio became popular. Papers all over the country engaged in fierce competition for readership. One of their tools for adding subscribers was finding and publishing the most popular cartoon strips, like The Gumps, Gasoline Alley, Popeye and others. My dad and mom, like many other readers, faithfully followed the antics of their favorite characters. Comic strips were the printed version of the "soap operas" that flooded the radio air waves during the depression days of the 1930s. The comics could also be called the television sitcoms of today.

My first awareness of these cartoons, before I was even able to read them, was when my mom and dad followed "The Nebbs" in the Herald Examiner, and even cut out and saved some of the strips.

When I investigated the stories behind the popularity of newspaper comics I learned that The Nebbs strip was a copy, or at least another version, of The Gumps, one of the longest running comic series. The Gumps appeared from 1917 to 1959. The strip was written and drawn by Sidney Smith, who lived in Barrington, the town where I was born. One of Smith's sons was well known as a stuck up kid and when I heard about his reputation I began to dislike The Gumps.

The source of The Gumps is interesting. The idea came from Joseph Patterson, editor and publisher of the Chicago Tribune. Although my dad did not like the Trib because of its Republican politics, it was, and still is an important paper in an important city. Patterson referred to the masses as "Gumps" and thought a strip about the domestic lives of common people and their ordinary activities would appeal to the average American newspaper reader. The Gumps were supposed to be very common, average folks. In the story line, the father, Andy Gump, was chinless and a bombastic blowhard. He was henpecked by his wife Min (Minerva) and their sons Chester and baby Goliath. Rich Uncle Bim showed up from time to time as did their annoying maid Tilda.

In real life I had never known anyone like Andy Gump. I thought the drawings were very crude and wondered why he had no chin. Then I learned Andy was a cartoon copy of a man Smith knew in real life, a man who lost his chin because of an infection resulting from a tooth extraction. I couldn't make a connection between the real man and Andy because I never felt cartoon strip characters were anything but pen and ink drawings, they never came to life for me. But for the general public, I suppose Sidney Smith did breathe life into his characters. As an example of how popular and real comic strips were, I read once that the May, 1929 strip about the death of a Gump's character, Mary Gold, caused a national sensation.

Smith became very wealthy. Since he lived nearby most Northbrook people knew about his lavish life style. One day when I was 14 dad read in the Herald Examiner that shortly after signing a contract, giving him $150,000 a year, on the way home Smith crashed his new Rolls-Royce and died in the head-on collision at the age of 58

When I was 12, in the 6th grade, I created my own cartoon character, "Moldy Moe", and drew sketches of Moldy in a car with huge wheels and tires. Calling someone "moldy" was, in those days, a mild insult to a person's mental abilities. I could never think of a funny story line for Moldy. I was always more interested in real life than fantasy and my humor more related to irony than slapstick. I also realized the truth too. Moldy was too much like Barney Google, another well known, very popular, cartoon character.

Another comic strip I remember more clearly than others was Moon Mullins because Moon reminded me of one of my uncles, my mother's younger brother John. John was a Chicago fireman who got fired because of drinking on the job. As a boy I knew of heavy drinking people and thought of them as very low class. But I still followed Moon in the daily paper. The Moon Mullins strip depicted the lives of diverse lowbrow characters who reside at the Plushbottom boarding house. The central character, Moon, short for Moonshine, is a so-called prizefighter, always out of cash.

Moonshine was a popular name for illegal whiskey. It came from the notion that prohibition alcohol was distilled "by the light of the moon". Bootleggers were so-called because men would sometimes tie flat pints of whiskey on their legs above their ankles which gave the appearance that they were wearing boots. Some bootleggers made a lot of money. John F. Kennedy's father, Joe Kennedy, was making the family fortune hauling whiskey from Canada to the United States while I was growing up during Prohibition.

Although Moon was tough-talking he was generally a good natured kind of guy. No doubt Moon was a horrible role model for any kid, but I knew he wasn't real and somewhat hilarious in a way. His adventures included stints in jail, stolen cars and failed employment opportunities. His little brother KO, who slept in an open dresser drawer, was a wise cracking smaller version of Moon. At the time I knew a real family with a couple kids who actually did sleep in big dresser drawers instead of beds.

Moon was created by cartoonist Frank Willard and Moon and his family had a 67 year run, from June 19, 1923 to June 2,1991. I liked Moon but thought Barney Google, a strip about another loser and his race horse "Sparkplug", who never won any races, was funnier. Since Barney was probably my inspiration for my own strip idea, Moldy Moe, I kept close track of Barney's and Sparkplug's antics.

"Bringing up Father" was also a comic strip I looked at every day. I can't remember why it appealed to me. Maybe the character "Jiggs" reminded me of one of my father's friends. Many readers simply called the strip "Maggie and Jiggs" after its two main characters. Bringing up Father was created by cartoonist George McManus. The humor centers on Jiggs, an immigrant Irishman and former hod carrier who came into wealth in the United States by winning a million dollars in a sweepstake. Now, newly rich, Jiggs still longs to revert to his former working class habits and lifestyle. He was constantly attempting to sneak out with his old gang of boisterous, rough-edged pals, eat corned beef and cabbage and hang out at the local tavern. But Jiggs' antics were always thwarted by his formidable, social-climbing, and rolling-pin wielding wife, Maggie. They had a lovely young daughter, Nora, and lazy son, Ethelbert.

Maggie is portrayed as a middle-class Irish American, desiring assimilation into mainstream society, while Jiggs is a more raffish "shanty Irish". Maggie's lofty goal, frustrated in nearly every strip, is to bring father, the low brow Jiggs, "up" to upper class standards, there for the title, "Bringing up Father". For some reason I could relate to Jiggs, probably because our family was first and second generation Swedes and many of our friends and neighbors were immigrants and second generation too.

When I was a boy, ethnic jokes abounded and were generally good natured. I heard some Irish people refer to their poor as Shanty Irish, and in the large Chicago Polish neighborhoods Pollock was their common designation. Swedish people were sometimes called Dumb Swedes, probably by Norwegians and Danes. No one took offense.

In today's "politically correct" atmosphere, Jiggs might be considered unacceptable as a stereotype. From my experience, people were much more open minded during the cartoon heyday. McManus was himself a full blooded Irishman who often dressed in the costume worn by Jiggs in the strip. Jiggs and Maggie were generally drawn with circles for eyes, a feature more often associated with another strip, "Little Orphan Annie".

Later strips like Peanuts and Pogo were bland by comparison to Moon Mullins and Jiggs. I did like Peanuts and Pogo, who had many humorous animal friends in the swamp. Doonesbury's political satire was lost on me. I was more inclined to favor Dick Tracy or Krazy Kat. In later years the comic strip drawings became more like illustrations than cartoons. "Terry and The Pirates" and "Steve Canyon" by Milton Caniff are the best examples and both were very popular. But by that time I wasn't interested in them and had gone back to preferring repeats of "The Katzenjammer Kids" and "Toonerville Trolley".

The Katzenjammer Kids were originally read to me when I was very young by my grandmother, my mother's mom who was called "Henny" for some reason. Henny was not as familiar with the English language as some other immigrants and often substituted Swedish words for the ones in the strip. But I could follow along and liked the Kids Hans und Fritz.

Their German was mangled some times but I didn't know the difference although I had learned some German words listening to the immigrants working on the peony farm. My words were most often those not heard in polite company because the workers were pretty rough fellows and my mother had to keep an eye on me when we had company.

Many popular comic strips were brought to life on the radio when broadcasting became more common. Writers and producers, as well as cast members, of those programs became local celebrities because most, if not all, the radio programs were produced in Chicago.

V

During the 1920s Prohibition was the law of the land. However, even we kids knew the names of all the local bootleggers. One prominent supplier was called Shotgun Louie, although I never learned the reason for the nick name. Louie supplied Northbrook residents and probably other communities as well with illegal moonshine. The suppliers of illegal booze were not all honest people. A girl I went with told me one time that her father bought a gallon of bootleg booze. Her dad checked the contents for quality and found it was OK. What he didn't learn until it was too late was that the can had a double bottom. On top, in a small part of the can, was the whiskey, but the other bigger section was filled with water to give correct weight.

Prohibition was a reform measure of the Progressive Social Causes Movement. Progressives wanted government solutions for social problems. A primary goal of the Prohibition Movement was the reduction of drinking by workers. The Progressives were helped by part of the business community who wanted sober, stable workers in order to increase production. The Prohibition Political Party was formed in Chicago, Illinois. Protestants were the major force for the "dries", while Catholics and Germans were the principal opponents of Prohibition, which was the 18th Amendment to the US Constitution.

When repeal of the 18th was proposed my dad, although not a heavy drinker, was in favor of repealing the Amendment. He had a bumper sticker on the Ford that read, "Repeal the 18th Amendment". He parked in the church lot where many of the church goers were against repeal. During the Great Depression many people in Northbrook, as well as Chicago and suburbs, were new immigrants, first generation Americans, like my mom and dad and most parents of my school friends. Northbrook people were definitely in favor of repealing the 18th Amendment. The 18th actually did not prohibit the private possession or drinking of alcoholic beverages. Many home owners brewed their own beer. My grandfather also made dandelion wine.

On Christmas Eve during the early years in the 1920s we would drive the 1924 Model T into Chicago to my mother's parent's home. My grandparents lived at 645 North Monticello Avenue in an area known as the Garfield Park District. Today that residential neighborhood has been turned into a slum with vacant lots and abandoned homes and has become one of Chicago's major drug centers. But when my grandparents lived there it was a comfortable combination Swedish and Italian neighborhood.

We had our Christmas dinner with my family, grandparents, uncles and uncle's wives on the evening before Christmas. It is the Swedish custom to have the main dinner Christmas Eve and set aside Christmas Day for relaxing when kids played with their holiday gifts. Presents were opened Christmas Eve. Many of the presents my brothers and I received were either educational or involved mechanical assembly, like an Erector Set or Tinker Toys. The first consisted of flat metal strips of various lengths with a number of holes in them. There were also prefabricated shapes and a small electric motor. The kit also contained small nuts and bolts and some washers and clamps. The purpose was to build towers, windmills, buildings and even an automobile, using the motor to operate what we had constructed. Tinker Toys did almost the same thing but with wooden sticks and round spools. The spools had several holes the sticks could be inserted into. An instruction book containing suggestions and pictures of things that could be built came with each kit.

Swedish Christmas dinners were big meals, including lutefisk and Lingonberries in whipped cream for desert. Lingonberries are to Scandinavians what blackberries are to Americans. They are tart, red berries, smaller and juicier than cranberries. Lingonberries grow wild on a short evergreen shrub in Sweden. My parents were used to them in the old country and my brothers and I enjoyed them too, with plenty of whipped cream. Maybe the desert was the reason we always slept on the way home after dinner.

Two incidents regarding Prohibition Era drinking stick out in my mind. One night as we drove down Chicago Avenue toward Monticello we could see several drunken people reveling on the sidewalk. I had never seen a drunken person before and my mother was disgusted at the sight of men staggering and leaning against buildings and street car stops on Christmas Eve.

Another incident that involved drinking was at Northbrook Days, an annual civic celebration held every August. I remember seeing the older brother of a friend of mine down in the dirt attempting to separate two fighting dogs. It was so funny it has stuck in my mind to this day, the swirling dirt and the dogs rolling with this guy in the middle. No one was hurt and the dogs were seen later, playing by chasing each other around the grounds like dogs often do.

V I

In late 1927 when "boom times" were still booming, my dad quit his job at Northbrook Gardens after a disagreement with the owner, Paul Batty. By now dad had acquired seventeen acres of the wooded land adjoining the west side of Grove School where I had been attending classes for one year.

I still remember picnics with my parents, grandparents and baby brother Elmer in that grove of hickory and oak trees while we still lived at Northbrook Gardens.

Although dad paid a thousand dollars an acre, open land in that area soon dropped to one hundred dollars or less per acre during the Great Depression. One time a boy I went to high school with, Donald Hintz, told me his father also bought 17 acres in the same general area for seventeen hundred dollars during the depression. Mr. Hintz paid one tenth of what my dad paid for the same acreage, and Hintz's down payment was a mere twenty five dollars. The Hintz family had a chicken farm on their property. I'm certain dad knew all about what was happening to land prices and I know he took it all in his stride. My folks and Mr. and Mrs. Hintz were friends and my father was not a man who would be resentful of anyone's good fortune. He would congratulate them. Dad paid off the debt he had incurred at the higher cost but I know it was a struggle at times.

Since coming to this country from Sweden as a young man, my father had a fervent determination to own his own peony garden on his own land. Peony flowers are common and popular in Sweden. Dad's familiarity with the flowers and roots was no doubt the main reason he applied for the job at Northbrook Gardens. That job was a start in the right direction, but owning his own business was his ultimate goal. My dad was a staunch believer in America as a country where opportunities were unlimited, but also knew hard work was required to take advantages of what this country offered. Dad was willing to work hard to accomplish his goals and he did both. He worked hard and "made it happen'. He taught my brothers and me what we needed for success and we learned by example. In my case I didn't realized what I had learned by dad's example until I started my own ad agency, after failing at some rather unpleasant jobs.

The property dad bought had never been farmed. I do remember seeing a couple dairy cows grazing there once as we drove past. For many generations before European settlers arrived, our property had been an Indian camp ground, probably used by members of the Pottawatomi Tribe. Pottawatomi Indians had also occupied the Northbrook downtown area for many years prior to the white settlers coming. During the years we lived there we found an abundance of arrow heads and other Indian artifacts while cultivating the rows of peonies.

There was a slight hill on the northwest corner of our land. The light colored dirt of the hill broke through the generally rich black soil of the farmland property. My brothers and I imagined teepees and Indian campfires on that hill. Dad didn't use the hill for peonies or any of the evergreens and elm trees he planted. One summer we raised some potatoes up there but the crop was very poor. After the potatoes didn't grow well my brothers and I wondered if the Indians had put a curse on that hill.

In 1833 the Pottawatomi ceded their Illinois lands and moved to a place near Council Bluffs. Iowa. One of the Forrest Preserves near us was named Pottawatomi Woods.

Sometimes we kids would "camp" there for a day and roast potatoes in the big open fire place the Park Service had built. Most often we were too impatient to let them roast long enough and ended up eating half raw potatoes. But it was still a lot of fun. Camping without adult supervision is something most kids are not able to enjoy today. It was part of our lives and we made the most of it.

The Glenview State Bank in Glenview, Illinois financed dad's purchase of the property. Glenview was about 5 miles south of Northbrook. Before the depression many smaller banks were individually owned, often by very, successful businessmen. The owner and president of the Glenview Bank was a man named Rugan. Mr. Rugan also owned a farm supply store in Glenview. Many years later, my dad told me that my grandfather wanted to give him the entire seventeen thousand dollars, and when times really got tough after the stock market crash, he wished he had taken the money. I suppose he felt even more strongly about the offer when my grandfather lost his entire fortune during the market collapse.

When economic times worsened after 1929, many people in the market, like my grandfather, lost all they had invested and several landowners and homeowners went bankrupt. Many lost property, and too often their homes as well. It is no wonder the 1930s were called "Hard Times".

Our peony farm was located atop a moraine that was formed thousands of years ago when glaciers pushed up the land in a series of hills and valleys similar to ocean waves. The moraine on which our property was located was known as

The Park Ridge Moraine and also contained Grove School, the University Golf Club behind our property and the North Northfield Cemetery. The cemetery bordered our property on the west and was separated from us by an old broken down twisted wire fence. Beautiful multicolored wild flowers and very sweet wild strawberries grew along the fence during the summer. North Northfield Cemetery is one of the oldest in the mid-west. I saw several headstones with dates from the 1700s. The grave markers are mostly weathered sandstone but most dates are clearly visible.

From the cemetery the moraine ran rather steeply down hill west to Sanders Road a half mile away. To the east of our property the moraine sloped more gradually to Pfingsten Road, about a mile away and then up to another moraine about 4 or 5 miles distant. All during the years I was growing up on that property, and for many years later, I knew nothing about the geology of the area. I only learned about it when a book about Northern Illinois was published in about 1999. I wish now that someone had told me the interesting story of the glaciers and their effect on the Illinois farmland. During my youth our local neighbors were concerned solely with their farms and crops, my dad with building his businesses. The history of the region, or its geology, was of little or no interest to the local people I knew. Most were concerned primarily with the effects the Great Depression was having on their lives.

VII

Most of 1928, while the land was being prepared for the peony farm, and our new house was being built on the same property, we lived in an apartment on Shermer Avenue in Northbrook. The village had its own school system and I attended 2nd grade there.

Population in 1928 was still about one thousand. Northbrook School had its eight grades in a two story red brick building. An addition to accommodate a three year high school was added in the mid 1930s. More space was built in 1939 when the school became a four year high school. I was in the first graduating class in June that year. Northbrook School was located on Waukegan Road, a short walk north from a small business district on the corner of Shermer and Waukegan. The old school building is now a retirement home.

Soon after we moved into the apartment I started 2nd grade. Almost the first day in class we had a fire drill. Since I had never experienced the noise of the alarm and busy confusion of kids getting up and walking out during the middle of the morning, I ran all the way home. Later, my mother, I know she was trying to suppress a smile, explained what had happened and I went back to school. Kids were in recess then and no one seemed to have noticed my absence. Later that morning while seated at my desk, I watched in astonishment as the mother of my schoolmate, Ruthie

Schmidt, bent over Ruthie's desk with her very short "flapper" skirt exposing more than she realized.

Flappers were young American women in the 1920s who wore very shot skirts, bobbed their hair, danced to jazz music, drank gin and drove cars. Flappers had their origins in the liberal period of the Roaring Twenties, the social and political turbulence that followed the end of World War I. They often flaunted their disdain for what was then considered acceptable behavior. Flappers were seen as brash for wearing excessive makeup,

John Held, Jr. was an American cartoonist, famous for his drawings that clearly illustrated the Flapper Era. Held created cheerful art showing his characters dancing, motoring and engaging in fun-filled activities. His drawings defined the flapper era so well that many people are familiar with Held's work today. Held illustrated many covers for Life Magazine prior to its 1936 purchase by Henry Luce. One of my most clearly held memories are the drawings made by Held because for me they sum up the 1920s more than anything else I remember. I liked Held's flapper illustrations as a kid and consider them historical treasures today. Drawings made by Held after 1930 are not well known.

The Flapper period was actually short lived. I guess the coming of the depression was responsible. I don't remember my mother or any of her friends as Flappers. Flappers must have lived in Chicago, where they were probably girls my uncles dated, they were not in Northbrook.

After the second grade I didn't see Ruthie again until we were both in high school. She was as pretty as her mother and was later selected by the Chicago Photographers Association as Miss Nude of 1940. She was also the smartest kid in our class.

I got along very well with most all the other kids in Northbrook. A boy by the name of Eloff tried to bully me a couple times and I was a little afraid of him, but since I spent most of the summer watching our new house being built I never saw him again.

During my earlier days on this earth I was a very insecure kid and to this day do not know the reason. My insecurity came to the forefront in the second grade when my brothers and I were given pocket watches by our uncle John. The watches were Ingersoll windups which sold for a dollar so were often just called "Dollar Watches". Instead of the usual numbers on the face, these watches had a picture of a golf ball. I wanted so badly to be accepted by the other kids that I told the boys I had several watches of the same type and could get more for the other kids. To make sure the kids believed my story, I gave one boy my own watch. As I got older and found there were many things I could do that other boys could not do, my insecurity was replaced with self confidence.

By 1928 old muddy Shermer Avenue in downtown Northbrook had been paved and the wooden sidewalks replaced with concrete. Almost all downtown businesses were located along Shermer Avenue between the Milwaukee Railroad tracks downtown and Waukegan Road to the north.

The buildings were all very much alike, two story wooden structures, owned by people who conducted family owned businesses. The first floor contained the business and the upper floors were family living quarters. My high school mate Freddy Weisman's father owned Weisman's Tavern, situated at the center of the business district. Next door was Bernhardt's Hardware. The hardware store was interesting because it had a knotty wooden floor that was difficult to walk on. That was because the building was so old the softer wood had worn away, leaving the hard knots that tended to throw one off balance if not very careful. The owner, Mrs. Bernhardt, had a son named Wally who was one of the town drunks. Wally worked in the store with his mother, and since they lived next door to Weisman's it was an easy trip between the two businesses several times a day. He was very fat and we heard would walk into the tavern, lift his huge stomach on the bar, and say "fill 'er up".

On the other side of Weisman's, toward the railroad track, was the A&P store, one of the first grocery stores that later became known as Super Markets. Next door to the A&P, along the track was Northbrook's only drugstore in a newer style brick and concrete building. Upstairs above the drug store was Doctor Therian's dental office, as well as the office of Roland Rembey, the best known of Northbrook's two doctors. He was reported to have a drinking problem but was still considered a good doctor.

In 1928 the Milwaukee Railroad tracks through Northbrook didn't have either signal lights or gates. When a train was still in the distance the station master, Mr. Hipsley, would come out from the station or from a tiny shack that stood between the station and the street and stand along the track holding a long pole. On top the pole was a round sign on which was printed the word "Stop" on both sides. Mr. Hipsley who had a bad limp would position himself at the edge of the track as trains approaching one hundred miles an hour would fly past him as he stood just a few feet away with dust and dirt swirling in the train's wake. When a freight train was stopped in town and moving box cars to a siding Shermer Avenue traffic was often blocked for a considerable length of time. Then it was Mr. Hipsley's job to have the engineer move the train to allow cars and walkers through the intersection.

Forty or more years later, after being away from Northbrook for most of my life, I took a commuter train from Northbrook to Chicago and was surprised to see the current ticket agent was Mr. Hipsley's son who looked exactly like his father.

On the other side of the track, same side of the street as the drug store, was a building supply store that had a side track running off the main line. Side track was used for unloading supplies. Next door to the building supply business was Toby's Barber Shop. Toby, a short stocky fellow, was the owner and main barber, and also known as an amateur boxer. He competed and often won in the local boxing matches. Next door and the last business on the west side of the street was Melzer's Grocery. They competed successfully with the newer A&P by offering home delivery. My mother was a loyal customer of Melzers. Melzer's had a boy nicknamed Skeezix who was a little older than me. His sister Mildred was my 7th and 8th grade teacher at Grove School. I remember her clearly because as I was seated in the front row she would put her reference book down on the seat in front of me and as she bent over I never took my eyes away, but they were not on the book.

Across the street opposite Melzers was a three story brick building. The first floor was the location of Landwehr's Department Store. Other floors contained apartments. Although small for a department store, Landwehr's seemed to offer everything the people in Northbrook needed. I remember they had a clothing department and every time my mother went shopping she found what she wanted at Landwehr's. They even had a complete soda fountain, the only one in town. The general manager was Eddie Griece, who was Landwehr the owner's son-in-law. Eddie's wife Irma also worked in the store and was very busy every time I went in there. The Grieses knew everyone in town because everyone had been a customer at one time or another.

There was a lot of train traffic on the Milwaukee Line in those days. Frequently, a long freight with as many as one hundred cars would stop traffic for awhile. Other times a speeding, non-stop, long distance passenger train would roar through town, just a few feet from Landwehr's Store. It must have been very noisy in those apartments. Even local trains that stopped at the station would rattle and clank and the hissing steam from the engine made a great deal of noise around the station.

Once in awhile during the one year we lived in town I would stand alongside the track as a slow mail train went past and watch the men working inside the mail car. As the train would ramble by I developed a strong longing to be on board, headed to some far off fabulous place where I envisioned fabulous adventures would be waiting just for me. I seemed to have been born with a desire to travel.

When I was in my first year in high school I used to ride to classes with a neighbor, Emil Maihack, who took his two daughters, Dorothy and Grace to school in a 1934 Chevrolet. Since we drove the same road at about the same time every school day, we often had to wait at the crossing where the Milwaukee tracks crossed Dundee Road, as a fast flyer came down the track. As I sat watching the train passing in front of me my imagination went soaring. Watching the powerful steam engine's drivers moving back and forth pushing the train to speeds nearing a hundred miles an hour was a stirring sight. Black smoke that came from the smoke stack hung in the air long after the train had passed. In the early morning semi-darkness the bright lights of the elegant dining car represented a world far different than mine, and I longed to be aboard that train. I kept my secret to myself. Sitting in Maihack's car I never dreamed that someday I would run a publishing company that would require four years of constant travel throughout the entire United States for me and my wife. I never got over the need to be on the move, and as a teenager

I hitch hiked to many different parts of the country during summers when I wasn't working in the peony fields.

But now the reality is Northbrook in 1928 and my description of down town. On the other side of the double track, same side as Landwehrs, was the tiny shack where Mr. Hipsley stayed most of the time when he wasn't needed in the main station and where he kept his "stop" pole. There was a parking lot next to Mr.Hipsley's shack where a couple Railroad Express wagons stood next to the station. Continuing north along Shermer Avenue, and next to the parking lot and station, was Lorentz's blacksmith shop. The owner, a short burley German, whose face bore the effects of smoke and heat from his profession, was often seen outside the front of his shop in his huge leather apron, conversing with passers by. He was always very friendly with kids who sometimes needed help fixing their bicycles. Sometimes he would be seen pumping gas from one of the two ancient pumps that were located right on the street in front of his shop.

There were a couple more buildings after the blacksmith shop. I don't remember what businesses they contained, but right next to the last was the Northbrook River that ran through the town's only park and baseball diamond. In summer, softball games were played there by competing teams from towns around the area. I was too young to be invited to join the Northbrook team although I really enjoyed playing baseball. When I was old enough to play, the games were no longer played. It seemed people had developed other forms of entertainment. One was free outdoor movies. In Glenview there was a big park named Roosevelt Park where three or four nights a week movies would be shown on a huge outdoor screen. Viewers brought their own folding chairs or simply sat on the grass. I went only a few times and don't remember if the movies were good or bad, but they were old ones. Northbrook Park was also where Northbrook Days celebrations were held each August. I have many memories of Northbrook Days, most very pleasant. Each year the celebration committee held a raffle, the big prize being a new car. In 1928 the winner was a 17 year old boy. As far as I know he kept the Chevrolet Roadster most, if not all his life. I know for certain he still had the car in the 1960s.

On the other side of Shermer Avenue the river came down along the Milwaukee tracks and ran under Shermer and through the park. We kids used to hike along the river and pick up stones to throw at the freight train box cars as they came down the track. There were many hobos "riding the rods" in those days but we were careful not to throw at them because the trains were often slow moving and we were afraid the hobos might jump off and come after us.

A huge house with a big tower on the 2nd floor was located on the corner of Shermer Avenue and Church Street. It was the home of Edgar Wessling, the main janitor at Northbrook High when I attended in 1939. He had two daughters, Virginia and Roma. In 2013 I was searching on Google Earth for some familiar landmarks in Northbrook. I ran the scanner up Shermer Avenue, now called Shermer Road. (probably its original name). There I saw the Wessling home, looking like it was well maintained, with a sign indicating it was one of Northbrook's historic land marks.

A block east of Wessling's house, on Church Street and Chapel Court, was the small church we attended while we lived at Northbrook Gardens. In 2013, 88 years later, the church was still there and looked exactly as I remembered it.

From Church Street, Shermer Avenue continues north where it intersects with Waukegan Road. A block north on Waukegan Road was the Northbrook School where I attended the 2nd grade and my first, second and senior years in high school. My third year was spent at Highland Park High School. The city of Highland Park is northeast of Northbrook on the edge of Lake Michigan. Before the fourth year was added to Northbrook High, most students went to Highland Park their last year, if they continued their schooling. Very few Northbrook students attended a college or university during the years we lived there..

On the west side of Shermer, almost at Waukegan Road was the apartment where we lived on the second floor while our peony farm home was being built. Next door to the apartment was an abandoned wooden barn with the front door gone. I explored the place along with a girl from school who gave me one of her figs from a bag. I had never even seen a fig before. It was very tasty.

Alongside the barn was a gravel driveway that led to a big old house with multicolored windows. From the sidewalk it looked like the haunted house one might see in a movie. A very rich but eccentric old man named Battack lived in it.

Apparently he lived there alone. It was said that at one time he owned much of the land that was included in the town of Northbrook, at that time called Shermerville. He always looked dirty and in warm weather didn't wear any shirt, but had a great big diamond stickpin stuck in the buttoned vest he wore. He never talked to any of us kids and nobody was afraid of him, although he was often seen nearby. None of us ever went near his big scary looking house either. Battack was just one of the many local characters found even today in small town America.

During the summer of 1928 I began going with my dad to the property where our new house was being built. I became acquainted with Teddy Marbet and his older sister Mary who lived on the east side of Grove School. Their parents ran a combination gas station and small café called Mary's Place. What I'm going to write might sound made up but is true; they had a hanging sign that read "Eat Here and Gas Up". Customers bought gas from the two-pump station by using a big lever to pump the gasoline up into a glass container on top of the pump. Then gravity sent the gas down into the car's gas tank. There was also a big red square tank that contained a reserve of motor oil which was pumped into individual glass jars that had metal spouts. I had seen Teddy and Mary once before. Both went riding past me on the street in town standing up in the back of my dad's model T truck. They had been over watching the construction of our house and my dad invited for a ride to town.

The house that was being built for us was a wood frame building, typical of the homes of the 1920s and 30s. My dad designed the two story house with a full basement himself and was careful that the contractors didn't change anything. My mother said he made one mistake because there were not enough closets. More were added later. There were six bedrooms, three on the first floor and three on the second. The second floor also had a large storage room at the front of the building. There was a single bathroom. The basement could be accessed from the kitchen as well as the back porch.

Beside the large kitchen the first floor contained a dining room and living room and front door to the outdoor porch. The living room had a huge red brick fireplace with bookcases on each side. Later the front porch was enclosed with glass.

A hallway dividing the bedrooms from the other first floor rooms ran down the center of the house. At one end was the stairs to the second floor. The other end held a big closet. The hall contained the entrance to the bathroom as well as the bedrooms. Mom and dad had the wall between two bedrooms knocked down to make one larger bedroom for themselves.

The out sides of the house were covered with grey shingles which were later painted red. Unfortunately the electrical wiring was very poorly done and the whole house had to be re-wired.

It was a well built and comfortable home but for some reason, which I could never understand I was ill at ease in the house in later years.

In the backyard was an underground room with the water pump and electrical controls. An iron lid covered the ladder down to the pump room.

VIII

Northbrook's history goes back a long way. Its downtown is located on a piece of land originally bought by a man named Joel Sterling Sherman. He bought the land for his family home, 159 acres for $1.25 an acre. Later, Frederick Schermer donated some land he owned for use as the first railroad station, named Schermer Station. Later the spelling was changed to Shermer Station and the community was named Shermerville after him, but only after a close referendum for incorporation in 1901. It was a farming community and at the time of incorporation the village had 311 residents and 60 houses. Shermerville also had five saloons, a meat market, a coal and feed store, a general store, a harness shop, a stonecutter, and the railroad station.

Shermerville gained a great deal of unwanted notoriety during its early years. The town was known for its boisterous gatherings of rowdy town ruffians at its inns and taverns. By 1921 the village's reputation had become so bad that residents believed the name should be changed. A renaming contest was held, and a man named Edward Landwehr submitted the name "Northbrook". In 1923, one year before we arrived,

Northbrook, the winner was adopted. By then the town had 500 residents. When my family moved there in 1924 not much had changed, and the town's reputation had improved only slightly.

One of the surviving Inns from the Shermerville-to-Northbrook days was Northfield Inn on Waukegan Road and Shermer Avenue. It was a wooden three story bar and restaurant that had once been a stage coach stop on the road between Chicago and Milwaukee, Wisconsin. Northfield Inn survived two World Wars, the Great Depression and because of its historical significance was saved for demolition and moved to the center of town in the 1980s. It is now the headquarters of the Northbrook Historical Society.

After the big Chicago Fire of 1871, brick had replaced wood in the city as the major construction material. So when a farm near present day Lake-Cook Road and Waukegan Road was found to have excellent clay soil for brick making, the National Brick Company and the Illinois Brick Company began their businesses. Most people I knew just called both companies The brick Yards since they were located close together. But some referred to National Brick as NBC. My dad knew a man who was employed there who told people he worked for the National Broadcasting Company. Dad did not like people who were liars, especially if they were doing it to impress people. From that I learned to keep people a little in the dark, a bit of mystery is better in relationships than letting people know everything about yourself.

For many years the two brick companies were assured a steady market. Both were located just north of Dundee Road, about a mile from downtown Northbrook. In 1872 a single side track was laid and the Chicago, Milwaukee & St. Paul Railroad began to haul the bricks to Chicago and other parts of the country. A second track was added in1892. Brick production peaked between 1915 and 1920, when as many as 300,000 bricks were manufactured a day. Many Northbrook men earned a living for themselves and family working in the Brick Yards.

The bricks produced in both yards were very high quality and there was a new demand for them many years later when they sold for premium prices as Chicago's old brick houses were torn, down making way for even newer building material. The brick yard companies were both still in full operation most of the time I lived in the Northbrook area, but by the1950s had closed.

When the brick companies moved away they left big holes where the clay had been dug. Many of the older boys used to go swimming in the Clay Holes and I know at least one boy drowned in one.

The brick makers established a residential settlement near the yards known as Bach Town. Many of the kids I went to school with, including Edward Bach, lived in Bach Town. The settlement was about a mile from Northbrook on Dundee Road about a mile east of our peony farm. Bach Town had only a couple short unpaved streets going south from Dundee Road. Almost all residents lived right on Dundee. Edward's family lived on the only farm in Bach Town. I don't know the population, but about 20 or so families lived there when I went to grade school and high school with many, if not all of the kids in Bach Town. I dated a couple of the BT girls. One was Lillie Theroux who was also my mother's part time maid. The Theroux's had several kids. I remember how annoyed my mother became when an older friend of mine, Joe Caldwell, tried to sneak into Lillie's room. Joe was never successful.

Our new family home was ready for occupancy by mid summer1929 and we moved in, although there was still some construction going on. Dad was building a large garage behind the house. He always called it "the barn".

Dad named the peony farm Glenbrook Gardens because of its proximity to both Northbrook and Glenview. Shortly after we moved in, dad sold an acre behind the school to the School District, which I'm sure helped our family's finances. Grove School kids used that additional land for a baseball diamond and the location of swings, slides and see-saws.

We boys used to roll old tires through the dust pretending we were cowboys and the tires were our trusty mounts. We called ourselves after our favorite movie cowboys. Alden Lindgren was Hoot Gibson and I was "Hoppy" after Hopalong Cassidy.

I was in the third grade and now was next door to the school so I no longer walked with the other kids like I did during my first year. My third grade teacher, who boarded with us, was Selma Bennett. Miss Bennett, as we were obliged to call her, later married my mother's cousin Martin Lofgren. I kept in touch with the Lofgren's for many years.

On the property, my father and hired hands spent over a year cutting down the massive oak and hickory trees, clearing the land for the peony flower business. As a result of the tree removal we piled up a supply of wood for the fireplace that lasted for many years. When we first moved in, and for a couple years afterward, my dad rented the unused land to local farmers and the fields around the house were filled with rows of corn stalks each summer..

Dad now began the main job of planting rows of peony plants on the acreage to the west of the house. He also laid out a show garden with flower beds between paths of grass. In the beds he planted samples of the various peony varieties. He took orders during summers when peonies were in full bloom and delivered the roots in the fall, the only time peonies can be transplanted successfully. The plants thrive best and their blooms are larger after a cold winter.

It takes one year before the plants bloom the first time and three years before blooming enough to be cut for commercial sale. It was my job during the summer to cut down the weeds between the rows of peonies. I detested that job.

The peony season begins in late May, with full bloom during June. But before the peonies are cut they need to be de-budded. This has to be done quickly, so a small army of men and women would descend on the fields to do the work. To de-bud a flower means removing all the side buds from the stem, allowing all the growth to go into one dominant bud. This produces a larger flower.

Almost all peonies are picked and sold to florists while the main flower is still a bud. After picking, the bottom leaves have to be stripped away, the stems gathered in bunches, usually in dozens, and tied with string in two places using a tying machine. Then bunches have to be put in a cool place to wait for pick-up. The coolest place for the bundled peonies was our basement where there might be eight or nine hundred bunches awaiting the florists. But they weren't there very long because this was a busy time for florists as well as peony growers.

The picking and bunching was done outdoors so soon the edge of the fields would be littered with leaves that had to be continually removed by truck. All this had to be done quickly, working long hours, because the season was short, often averaging less than a month. Some peonies picked while in bud would be placed in cold storage for sale later in the year. My dad rented cold storage space in Chicago. Flowers in full bloom were sold from the drive-up stand dad had built on Dundee Road.

For several months during the summer the show garden, where individual varieties were planted, was very busy with people who grew peonies in their own gardens. Customers would select their favorites for delivery in the fall. Fall was a busy time too because the roots had to be dug before the ground became frozen.

The show garden had metal sticks with wooden blocks attached identifying the peony name and variety. It was often my job to repaint the blocks because the hot sun would obscure the names. I would do this in the winter after school.

During the fall, before the ground became frozen, the peony roots of the varieties that had been ordered during the summer were dug, split apart and shipped. This was a very precise job that dad handled personally. The roots all looked pretty much alike and could easily be mixed up, so the work of shipping extended into the winter months.

What my brothers and I liked best of all was when the old peony foliage was cut and burned. This was a bigger job than just for family work, so crews of men did most of the job. They would cut the old peony stems at ground level with hoes or clippers. Then the leaves would be raked into huge piles and set on fire. This was the part we liked best. On cold days, standing next to the fire was pleasant, until our backs got cold. Then we would turn around with backs to the blaze.

This work went on for quite a few days and the October air was filled with light smoke and the very pleasing smell of burning shrubbery. The odor was very similar to the pungent smell of burning leaves in the cities of the Midwest, leaves that were raked into the gutters and set on fire. In Chicago my grandparents also had a big square concrete pot in the alley behind their house for burning rubbish. None was hauled away. Getting rid of leaves and rubbish this way was an important part of mid western life during the 20s and 30s.

Chicago alleys were also used by men selling ice, fish,

poultry, bakery goods and almost everything the home owners would buy and use. As I remember, the seller's wagons were always pulled by a single horse, usually an ancient nag who stood patiently by as sales were made. In the summertime, neighborhood kids would go out and pet the horses and give them a treat, most often a sugar cube or an apple.

During most of the depression, we also grew beans, peas, radishes, peppers, carrots, beets and other vegetables for ourselves and for sale at the roadside stand. With an orchard to provide many kinds of fruit, we always had a plentiful supply of good food we grew ourselves. We didn't have a cow, but bought milk and butter from one of the farms or from Melzer's Store in town.

One time my dad had a chicken house and yard built and bought a flock of white leghorn chickens. He believed local farm eggs came from chickens that were poorly fed. So he bought his own grain and mash and mixed it himself. The problem was, eggs from the farm or store were ten cents a dozen while eggs from his specially fed hens cost near a dollar. That experiment soon ended. One day a big truck showed up and the leghorns were sold, loaded up and hauled away. Another problem with that type chicken was that they had a tendency to take wing and fly out of the yard. Only very high fencing kept them in.

When the hens and one rooster were gone, the chicken coop became a tool shed. I was glad too, because feeding and cleaning the chicken roosts had often been my job. I learned chickens were either stubborn or fiercely independent because

I had a hard time getting them in the coop when they wanted to stay in the yard.

Another time we had some rabbits. One day when dad thought it was too hot for them upstairs in the garage we let them out of their pens to run around the cars downstairs where it might be cooler. Then someone left the garage doors open and the rabbits got out. There was no use trying to round them up so they ran around in the neighborhood fields and soon mixed with the wild rabbits. For 20 years we would see rabbits with diverse colors, some with black and white blotches in with the grey fur of the wild ones.

While we lived a typical country life on the peony farm, my two uncles, who lived in Chicago with mother's parents, often referred to us as "county bumpkins'. But the truth was we were most fortunate to live in the open fresh air, far away from the coal smoke and grime of the city.

Our mailing address was Northbrook and our mail was delivered from the Northbrook Post Office to our mail box on a pole on Dundee Road. We were considered residents of the Northbrook community. But just a mile and half west of our home was the small town of Wheeling. Wheeling was closer to us than Northbrook but the stores and businesses we frequented were in Northbrook. The kids in Wheeling went to their own school through the 8th grade but attended high school in Northbrook.

We knew many Wheeling families and my brother Elmer married Betty Schmidt from Wheeling.

The Wheeling business district was located north and south of Dundee Road along Milwaukee Avenue. The property on the east side of Milwaukee Avenue was backed up by the Des Plaines River. There were some small taverns in Wheeling where I went with my dad a few times. I remember I thought the bars smelled foul and were always full of smoke. But we never stayed long because dad was not much of a drinker and he was usually there talking with some business acquaintances.

There were a couple good restaurants in Wheeling. One was the Hartman House located on the edge of the river. It was well known but the most popular was the Union Hotel. Every Friday the Union Hotel had a big fish-fry night. Lake Michigan is famous for a good supply of Perch, a great fish and very tasty when fried in butter. Northbrook also had fish-fry night every Friday at the American Legion Hall. That tradition continued well into the 1950s. I went often but never thought about drinking any beer which was in plentiful supply at both places.

Around both Wheeling and Northbrook where many Germans lived there were some big German beer halls. The most popular was Schufreiders . The place was enclosed by huge green wooden walls. As customers approached they could hear the German band playing with lots of oom pa horns. The music put everyone in a good mood. It was all very colorful and festive. The kids just ran around the grounds while their parents enjoyed the good German beer. For some reason, maybe because of the kids, the Beer Halls were never open very late.

IX

In early 1929 there were few people who thought business would not continue its upward expansion. In those days parents did not discuss the family's monetary affairs with their kids. I was never fully aware of the financial arrangement my father made establishing and operated our peony business during the hard times that were coming. When I was about 15 I got my first impression of trouble when my mother's parents came to live with us. I suspected something was wrong because they had lived in a fine middle class home in Chicago. Since I was the oldest grandchild they had always lavished gifts on me. I only knew as an adult that grandfather had lost all his money in the stock market..

People in the Roaring Twenties seemed to think everyone could get rich "playing the market". Sometimes it worked that way. A stock bought one day might be sold a couple days later at a profit. But soon people were buying stock on margin. That meant buying stock for as little as ten percent down. You could buy ten thousand dollars worth a stock for one thousand dollars. Sounded like a good deal. Only problem was if the stock went down the buyer had to come up with more cash to hold the stock. My grandfather sold his valuable properties when his stock went down in order to hold on to what he had bought. It was his belief, as well as all most everyone else, that soon the stock would regain its original value. The '29 crash came and he lost it all in the end.

I learned later that at one time my grandfather had owned much of the property in downtown Waukegan, Illinois. When mom's parents came to live with us they had already lost everything. He and many others had also lost a lot of money buying land in Florida that turned out to be valueless swampland.

I remember the serious look on my dad's face when he was reading the newspaper and commenting to my mother on his concern about what was happening. For bad stock market news had already begun in September, 1929, soon after we moved in the new house. But on Thursday October 24th, massive selling caused stock prices to drop dramatically as brokers could not find buyers to keep the stock prices stable. On Monday October 28th millions more shares were sold and the stock prices continued to fall until the market completely collapsed.

Despite this awful news dad was always optimistic about the future of his business and went ahead with putting tiles in the fields to drain off surplus water. He also had a pond dug behind the orchard. So far there was no change in our lives and we were living in a new house much larger than the one at Northbrook Gardens. But with the stock market crash in October, the country changed rapidly for everybody.

Eventually stock market investors saw a dramatic decline that not only left thousands of individual investors broke, the drop in the value of assets also put pressure on banks and other financial institutions. That was especially true of banks holding many rapidly declining stocks. While so far our personal lives had not changed much, all around us banks were being forced into insolvency which would soon affect everyone. By 1933, out of the United States' 25,000 banks 11,000 had failed. Unemployment had risen to about 25-30 percent of the United States' work force. My dad's investment was in the land on which he built the peony farm. His decision proved to be the best investment of all in the end.

There is one characteristic of the 1920s that some people argue had a severe impact later on. That was the great disparity of income and accumulated wealth that occurred during the Roaring Twenties. A large part of the reason for the growing gap between rich and poor was thought to be because of the increase in productivity between 1920 and 1929. But it still isn't clear whether that fact had a direct relationship to the depression. Still, the Great Depression was preceded by the so-called New Era, a time of low unemployment when general prosperity masked vast disparities in income.

In 1921, the year I was born, the country was in a slight recession but during the rest of my early years times were highly prosperous. Even as a kid I felt my life was pretty darn good.

One of the challenges in a consumer-driven economy like that of the United States is to convince people that they need to keep buying. And, by mid 1920 advertising had already become both an art and a science in selling products and services to consumers.

In its very early stages, traditional advertising merely suggested the availability of a product. By 1926, ads earnestly explained the necessity of a product, even when the necessity might be wholly fabricated. Normal health and hygiene conditions were elevated to serious sounding maladies. Bad breath became halitosis, sour stomach was acidosis, all of which were cured by some product or other.

When my own advertising agency was established in 1960, all that groundwork had been put in place for a long time. Our job in the 60s, 70s and 80s was to convince people who were already buying cars, to buy our client's brand.

My mother won a number of contests when she submitted advertising slogans and ideas to Chicago ad agencies during the 1930s. Had she wanted to do so, she could have been an excellent copywriter for any ad agency. I learned much of my copywriting ability from her. But in 1935 my serious interest in advertising was still far in the future.

Economist Stuart Chase had observed in 1925 that "advertising creates a dream world of smiling faces, white teeth, schoolgirl complexion, distinguished collars, wrinkle free pants and happy homes". All this was still true when I was in the ad business. In 1965 we had Mr. Clean, The Marlboro Man, Lux "The Soap of Beautiful Women" and cigarette testimonials by doctors and sports figures.

One of the most successful advertising practitioners I remember as a boy was Bruce Barton, head of BBD&O, an ad agency I admired. Barton wrote a best-selling book titled "The Man Nobody Knows". The book, which sold 700,000 copies, portrayed Jesus Christ as a super salesman and the father of modern business. I never read Barton's book and I am sure none of this was of any interest to my dad or any of his friends at this time.

Still, as the stock market continued to decline unemployment rose even more and wages fell for those who were still working. The use of credit for the purchase of homes, cars, furniture and household appliances resulted in foreclosures and repossessions.

I remember a boy in the same grade as I was in at Grove School who would often be driven to school along with his sister by their father in a fairly new Chevy. One day they showed up in an old Hupmobile. This kid's father had a succession of jobs and was one of the many people who had lost buying power as industrial production fell.

I noticed other kids in school wearing the same clothing worn by their older sisters or brothers the year before. In my case, I wore the same pair of Corduroy pants during my entire term at Highland Park High. Corduroy is a tough material and mine, even after several washings, looked as good at the end of the school year as at the beginning.

In Northbrook and other towns around us we saw empty stores of businesses that had failed, and more workers lost their jobs. No amount of advertising, mine or anyone else's, could have stemmed the tide of gloom sweeping the country.

In 1931 when the worst of the depression began I was 10 years old. As city dwellers lost their homes, the farmers around Northbrook were also caught in the financial squeeze, along with those in the rest of the country. Some soon lost their land and equipment to foreclosure. The Knoll's across the road from us sold some of their horses that were not needed on their farm. I remember going to auctions around the area with my dad. If dad bought anything he could use I don't know, but I saw several tractors and other equipment for sale at each farm.

President Herbert Hoover, a Republican and former Commerce Secretary, believed the government should monitor the economy and encourage "counter-cyclical spending" (whatever that meant) to ease downturns, but not directly intervene. As the jobless population grew, he resisted calls from Congress, governors, and mayors to combat unemployment by financing public service jobs. I heard Hoover on the radio encouraging the creation of such jobs, but said it was up to state and local governments to pay for them. I remember my dad saying that Hoover believed that relieving the suffering of the unemployed was solely up to local governments and private charities. What I remembered when hearing Hoover speak was that he had an unpleasant voice, or at least it seemed annoying to me.

We knew several families who were "on relief" at the time. What is now called welfare was known as relief in the 30s and administered by Cook and other counties.

Some times desperately hungry people would resort to catsup soup. Catsup soup was made by ordering hot water in a cup in a restaurant and while the waiter was not looking sneak catsup into the cup. It must have been pretty thin soup. That was extreme anxiety

One project begun in 1931 during Hoover's Administration was the gigantic Hoover Dam that brought water and electricity to the growing South West. Finished in 1936 after more than one hundred workers had lost their lives, the dam was dedicated by President Franklin Roosevelt who referred to it as Boulder Dam. A nearby housing project was named Boulder City. Later the dam's name was changed to its original Hoover Dam and is known by that name today.

When unemployment soared past 20 percent, thousands of banks and businesses had failed and millions were homeless, the notorious gangster Al Capone opened up "soup kitchens" for the homeless in Chicago. His smiling face was often seen pictured in the Tribune and Herald-American newspapers and many magazines. Capone got great coverage with every thing he did. Every day the newspapers were full of stories about Capone and the other Chicago Mobsters. Very often the news was about how Capone was able to use his money to control corrupt police and judges so they would dismiss cases against crime bosses. It was easy when growing up in and around Chicago to get the impression that we lived in a bad area, except I thought that was the way everyone in the country lived.

There was a great deal of news every day about the gang wars going one, particularly between the George "Bugs" Moran gang who controlled beer, gambling, speakeasies and prostitution on the North Side and Capone on the South.

Madison Street in Chicago was the dividing line. There were shootings and killings almost every day between these and other rival gangs. The worst was the St. Valentine's Day killing of seven Malone's men in 1929. Bugs Malone himself was supposed to be there but became suspicious and walked on past the building.

I don't remember even reading about the St. Valentine's Day Massacre but heard a lot of talk about it. Most people and the police believed Capone was responsible for the shooting by men dressed in police uniforms. Bugs was quoted as saying, "No one kills like that except Capone."

One time when I was in the neighborhood where it happened I walked up Clark Street to look at the building that was the crime scene. When I saw the door to the abandoned warehouse was open I went inside. The room was smaller than it looked in pictures and was very dark. I imagined bullet holes in the brick wall but there was no evidence of the murders that had happened there.

In the end Capone's money and influence didn't help him. The U.S. Government charged him with income tax evasion and when he was convicted sent him to Alcatraz Prison.

.

I remember seeing Chicago newspaper pictures of men and women coming home from fruitless job hunts to find their dwellings padlocked and their possessions and families turned into the street. These stories generally concerned people in Chicago itself, but the suburbs were little better. Many lived at the edges of cities in makeshift shantytowns.

I went to high school with two girls who lived in a make shift house built with plywood and 2 by 4s, with virtually no insulation. I thought it strange that their father would build that shanty so close to the fine brick house the family had lived in and lost. From the kitchen window they could see their former home, standing empty on a nearby hill. It was that bad for many others too.

As boys, my brothers and I heard about these awful conditions but the peony farm was bringing enough income so we were able to avoid many of these problems. Unknown to us, my father had to make arrangements for payments on the land that were different than his original agreement. The Glenview State Bank's owner, Mr. Rugan, like most bankers in those days, knew borrowers personally and felt dad was a good enough risk to make payment adjustments during these hard times.

Years later, when I was in high school, a girl who was Rugan's granddaughter was obvious in her hatred for me, and probably my brother Elmer too. Her mother was Rugan's daughter and during hard times the daughter wanted her father to foreclose on my dad's property and give the land to her and her husband. The granddaughter must have heard her parents talking about the property, which by then had become much more valuable than the vacant land dad bought originally. I could understand why they avariciously wanted the bank to foreclose. By high school days the peony farm was thriving and well known. I felt that was what made her dislike me even more. I forget why I never told my dad about her, and it wouldn't have changed anything if I had. For a long time I remembered the girl's name but eventually forgot.

X

In 1930, just as America was beginning to feel the full impact of the Great Depression, there were 43 kids enrolled in the eight grades in Grove School. I was now in the fourth and my brother Elmer was in the first grade that year. In the picture taken that fall, Elmer is seated back in the last seat in the first row. When the picture was shot I had already decided to be an independent individual. So I roughed up my hair and sat holding a wooden ruler up to my mouth. I definitely didn't want to look like the rest of the kids.

The teacher's desk was located in front, facing the student's desks. The wall behind the teacher was almost completely filled with a gigantic blackboard. Our desks were made of cast iron with wooden seats. Desk top was a writing table. Books and personal items were kept on a shelf under the desk top. Desk also had a small round hole in the upper right corner that contained a bottle of ink. All books and equipment were furnished by the school district and passed on to students from year to year.

Sometimes the seventh and eighth grade girls would help teach the younger children. The older girls would generally help first and second graders with their reading lessons and to complete simple arithmetic problems.

Toilets consisted of two rooms at the front end of the building, one for boys and one for girls. The utilities in the toilet rooms consisted of no more than a board with holes. There was an old fashioned outhouse back of the school but it wasn't used and was torn down soon after the school year started. A woodshed stood back there too. There was no running water. A cast iron pump was located near the building entrance. Drinking water came from the pump. Actually it was excellent water that came from a deep well.

The school was heated in winter by a single pot bellied stove at the entrance of the single room. There were cloak rooms on each side of the entrance door, for use just before we entered the school room itself. There was no telephone. Emergency calls were made from a neighbor's home. Some of the kids I went to school with were extremely poor and their clothing often reflected their parent's lack of income. Many families were on relief.

Grove School had a very interesting history. In 1833 a man by the name of Levi Kennecott settled with his brothers in the grove of oak, but mostly hickory, trees near or on the land my family now owned. On November 20th of the same year Kennecott deeded a small parcel of land for a school. It became School District 3 and opened for classes in 1853. Ten years later Grove School had 96 students, but the average daily attendance was probably half that number. Miss Anderson, the first teacher, was paid eighty dollars for the short season. Students went to school only in winter in earlier days because they were needed on the family farm the rest of the year. Mr. Kennecott was paid six dollars for boarding the teacher in his home.

I don't know if there is any record showing exactly where Kennecott's home was situated, but it must have been near the school since the teacher boarded with him. There was a small old frame house located just east of the school property. It was now the Marbet home and Café. Since Kennecott was so closely involved with the school, and was a director, that site, probably with a different building, may be where he lived.

In 1850 Northfield Township where the school was located had a population of 1,013. Almost all lived on farms. In 1886 the original school building was replaced with the one my brother and I attended in the 1930s. The cost was $224.95. School year was extended to eight months. Three years later term was nine months, which ended the long tradition of school in winter only. It was District 27 by then and remained that number to the end of its existence.

Much history was made in The United States during Grove School's years: The Civil War (1861-1865), Lincoln assassinated (1865), The Great Chicago Fire (1871), Bell' Telephone (1876) and Edison's light bulb (1879) were just a few of the historical events..

Our school day ran from 9am until 3:30pm. School lunches were unheard of so kids brought their lunches in lunch boxes, usually with milk in a thermos bottle in the rounded top. Kids would often trade sandwiches. "I'll give you my peanut butter for your jelly sandwich".

I ran home next door for lunch but hurried back to spend as much time as possible playing in baseball games during warmer weather, boys against the girls. The boys didn't always win. Mimi Reef was the girl's first baseman and a very good hitter. Her brothers Louis and Leonard were also good players. I was a fairly good hitter but a poor infielder. My brother was too young to play. In winter we engaged in snowball fights. Beside the hour for lunch the day was broken by two fifteen minute recesses.

The school had a well stocked library including the Book of Knowledge Series and I think I read every page in every book.

Grove School was so small that kids would play a game of throwing a ball over the roof to those waiting on the other side who would try to catch it. We couldn't see those on the opposite side throwing the ball so never knew when it was coming. Suspense was what made the game more interesting.

There were slides, teeter totters, swings, poles and a high pole with chains that held grip handles at the end. Kids would hang on and push the whole apparatus around in a circle. It was easy to get hit in the head and I don't think this one would be allowed today in our protective society. But it was the most fun in the playground. We didn't worry about a bump on the head. I got hit more than once.

The 1930s were years when lighter-than-air dirigibles were much in the news, especially the Navy dirigible Akron which crashed during a vicious storm off the New Jersey coast in 1933.

One day a huge dirigible came drifting very slowly just a few feet above ground over the vacant land across from the school. I was the first kid to rush out of class and across Dundee Road. Usually we were forbidden to cross the road during school hours but I knew this was an exception. It was a sight I will never forget. The silver monster filling the sky was a moment reserved for a very few fortunate kids.

The dirigible had almost come to a stop while we stood there spell bound. My brother Elmer says that even today the picture is still in his mind. A couple short ropes hung from the cabin but since there was no one on the ground to catch them I knew the ship was not going to land. We all waved at the men inside the cabin and they waved back.

Then the engines began to rev up and the giant picked up speed and started to rise as it moved forward. We would have waited until it was out of sight I guess, but Miss McLain called us back to class.

In 1935 Akron's sister ship, Macon, also crashed during a storm off Big Sure, California. Those crashes doomed the rigid dirigible's future in America. The Hindenburg's fiery explosion in 1937 ended the era.

Punishment for infractions at Grove School was sure and swift. When Louis Reeb and I were caught peeking through the door of the girl's toilet we were taken separately into the boy's room and paddled. Miss McLain may have been short but she had a strong arm. We were also required to take a note from the teacher to our parents explaining the infraction. That was the worst part of the punishment.

I have many memories of those Grove School days. One experience is a especially memorable. Grove was engaged in a baseball game with another grade school called the Maple School. Since I had to go to a church catechism class I was unable to play in the first part of the game. After class I rode my bike at top speed to get to play in the rest of the game. I rode my bike onto the school grounds in a cloud of dust with the kids cheering loudly. They thought, and I did too, that I would become the hero of the game because I was a fairly good player. I laid my bike down and was immediately put in at bat as a pinch hitter. My school was behind, but there were two on base, so here was a chance to become a star. In three pitches I struck out!

Of course there was no bussing in those days and all the kids walked to school, some as far as a couple miles. In the harsh Illinois winter one or two came to school with frozen noses and ears. A few days later they would have big water blisters where the tissue had been damaged, usually the lobes of their ears. I never knew of any other serious after effects or that any had medical attention.

One family had two girls and an adopted boy in school. The boy was in the 7th grade and drove to school in one of the family's cars. I started to drive when I was 13 but by the time my dad took me out to teach me I had already sat in the car in the garage practicing using the clutch and gear shift so the next day he let me drive alone.

In the fourth grade I had my first girlfriend. Her name was Marjorie Chestain, a sixth grader. The teacher reprimanded us for walking around the school yard with our arms around each other. Marjorie didn't go on to high school and as a teenager was killed in an automobile accident. There were other young people in the car and I heard drinking was involved. I never learned the fate of the others who were with Marjorie.

Not all was innocence in the schoolyard either. These kids lived on or near farms with all kinds of animals. They knew the score. I had undressed one of the girls at least once by the time I was in the 7th grade. (It wasn't Marjorie) An expression I heard often by girls who liked a certain boy they wanted to be with was, I want to have him "feel me up". A movie titled "The Vamp" came out about 1931. We didn't go to see it but Virgene Gilmore thought it was a compliment when some kids called Gene a Vamp.

A girl named Muller, I can't remember her first name, took me behind the school building where we leaned against the brick foundation and she showed me some pictures of naked women in a magazine she had sneaked out of her older brother's room. They weren't pornographic but art pictures in various poses. I asked the girl to get more pictures but she couldn't risk trouble with her brothers. Just then the teacher rang the bell, ending recess. The bell the teacher used was made of brass, about 8 inches in diameter. It had a black handle and sat on the teacher's desk. She would stand in the doorway and ring the bell to end lunch and recess, and in the morning to start school.

Kids in school knew all the other kid's parents too. June Johnson's dad was called "Windy" by the boys. John

Gilmore's father, Jack, got drunk at one of the parties at our house and lost his false teeth. He came back the next day looking for them and found them in a pile of sand. Some of the names kids called parent's friends weren't very nice. My brothers and I called dad's friend from Sweden, Swan Olson, Swine Olson, but we weren't malicious, just thought we were funny.

Another girl I liked was Ruth Ballack who I used to walk home from school every day when we were in the 5th and 6th grades. Ruth lived about 2½ miles away, down a gravel road past some farms, one with a nasty dog. Her home was located among a small group of houses where many of the other school kids also lived.

After leaving Ruth at her parent's house I would walk home again. It was a long walk, but not for someone in love. That nasty dog stayed in the yard as we walked past. But he hated bicycles and came running after me when I rode by the farm. I peddled faster than the dog could run but still worried because on the gravel road I might skid and fall. One day I skidded and did come to a stop. The dog that had been chasing me stopped too and stood looking at me. Then his tail began to wag so I patted him on top of his head. He had just been lonely and chased me for fun. From then on Ruth and I would stop and spend a little time with him each time we walked past the farm. We never saw the people who owned the farm. It must have been a lonely place for that dog.

Sometimes I would ride my bike a long way from home. I often rode to town and once in awhile as far away as the shore of Lake Michigan about 10 miles away. There was a park high above the beach where I would leave my bike and walk down a path to the water. Once I tripped and rolled head over heels down the entire trail. Although there was broken glass as well as stones and rocks on the path I didn't get hurt. But the front soles of both my shoes came apart and were flopping like a cartoon character's mouth. So I couldn't walk in the shoes and went back to the top in stocking feet. I could still ride my bike and I was very sore for a few days.

Ruth didn't go to high school, married and lived across the street from Northbrook High. Some times I would stop and talk with her on my way to football practice. We kept in touch with each other and as we grew older often talked of our fond memories of childhood days at Grove School.

There were 9 kids in my 8th grade graduating class. Three of the graduates did not go on to high school. I was the only one to attend college.

Most Grove School students spent their entire lives in Northbrook and other northern Chicago suburbs, married local people and settled down. I think all the boys served in the Armed Forces during the Second World War and Harry Ropenack lost his life serving his country.

I was a pilot in the Naval Air Corps when the war ended. My closest neighbor Teddy Marbet joined the Army about a year before the Pearl Harbor attack. I didn't see him again until I went to his mother's funeral after the war. Teddy had aged in appearance well beyond his actual years. I thought the change was because of experiences during his army service.

While others stayed around Northbrook I went west, eventually to Salt Lake City, Utah where I met and married Jean Daniels from Rock Springs, Wyoming, and eventually started my advertising agency. We had two children, Anita and Rhonda. After my wife Jean died I moved to Southern California and am now a writer and producer of educational videos for Discovery Education.

During the summer of 1933 the school district had the old one-room building turned around 90 degrees, moved it farther back from Dundee Road, added another room and basement. In 1951 a new Grove School was constructed on Pfingsten Road about a mile east of the old school and in 1952 classes began in the new school.

The days of Grove School on Dundee Road are long past. The site where Grove School stood is now covered by expensive homes. The farms across the road are now the huge Sportsman's Country Club and Golf Course.

In 2007, long after the school was gone, the Northbrook Historical Society published an excellent history of District 27, which was Grove School's official designation. I was asked to supply pictures which had been given me by my 4th grade teacher Vera McLain. These small black and white photos, taken in 1931, of kids in the playground in winter are all that remain of Grove School's existence. Now there isn't even a sign to mark the school's historic location. I hope some day to be able to erect a sign or something to designate the site of historic Grove School myself.

We few who are left will never forget those wonderful childhood days in one-room Grove School on Dundee Road, the school and its teachers who helped shape our lives forever.

Life in our home was typical of America in the 1930s. My dad ran the peony farm business and our house was on the same property. My mother, who had worked before marriage, was home for us all the time. She was, like all the mothers of our friends, wife, mother, homemaker and nurse. Only on rare occasions did she need to resort to the help of a doctor. One time was when I had my tonsils out at a small hospital in nearby Wheeling, The medical facility was owned by Dr. Larson. I suppose I was also treated there when I was four years old and severely sick with diphtheria. I remember the tonsillectomy, which was terribly botched but not the other illness. My brothers, Elmer and Paul, seemed not to have needed professional medical care that I remember. One time my dad was extremely ill with what was called Quincy Sore Throat, but recovered after a long bout with the illness. I remember he lost a great deal of weight which was quite noticeable because he was slender and tall by nature.

We ate all our meals together, except for the infrequent times when dad was away on business. We never ate supper until dad was home. If he was detained some place dad never failed to call my mother.

We always had a dog, generally a collie, and one or two cats. We never thought about dog or cat food: the animals ate the same food we did and were always healthy and active. I think most country dogs in those days died of old age.

We spent a great deal of time in the evening as a family, often listening to radio programs together. We boys were not allowed to listen to the radio until homework was completed.

I remember one radio we had was a Philco with a dial that could be set to receive shortwave broadcasts. Most of the stations broadcasting from overseas were based in London. Every New Years Eve one London station would broadcast sounds of the huge clock, Big Ben, tolling out the old and tolling in the New Year. Of course, because of the time difference, we heard Big Ben in early evening. We also heard Adolph Hitler after he had assumed control of Germany. The only person who could understand Hitler was my mother's father who had grown up in Germany. Grandfather never bothered to translate, but he had left Germany soon after 1918, the end of the Great War, before Hitler was even in the news.

My dad subscribed to several magazines and other publications as well as newspapers. Our book cases contained a plentiful supply of good reading material. What I liked best were the Tom Swift Books. One of my favorites was "Tom Swift and his Electric Runabout". The books were generally about Tom and his several mechanical apparatuses. These books allowed my mind to soar, hoping some day I too would work with these and other devices.

In high school I drew endless automobile designs. My goal then was to build a car manufacturing company like that of my idol Henry Ford. I even named my car the Corburn, a combination of Cord and Auburn, two cars famous for innovation and speed.

My friends lived lives similar to ours. I didn't know any kids whose parents were divorced or separated. All those I knew lived in homes on their own land. Many were farm homes and some farm families were large, often with six or more children.

When I remember holidays as a boy, they seemed more important to people in the 30s than holidays do today. We were out of school for both Lincoln's and Washington's Birthday. Independence Day was simply called "Fourth of July". Fire crackers were everywhere. We had little pieces of red stuff that looked like broken glass that we threw down on the sidewalk, or against a brick wall and they would sparkle and sound like a fire cracker. But the very best of all were the round Cherry Bombs, when we kids could afford them. Cherry Bombs would throw a tin can up into "outer space". And they were extremely loud. That was best of all. There were no restrictions on fireworks and I never heard of anyone getting hurt. We were very careful.

Before our grandparents came to live with us they would come out from Chicago to spend the 4th with us. My grandfather Muffa would bring an arm full of sky rockets that he would fire off from the show garden. Of course they had to be set off after dark to get the full effect. By then Muffa had had quite a bit to drink. My mother was always glad when the last rocket had gone off because Muffa wasn't too careful about which direction he aimed them. Mom was afraid a rocket might land of the roof of the house and start a fire. I'm certain the roof had fire proof shingles, but she was concerned never the less.

The really big holiday, as far as my dad was concerned, was Armistice Day, November 11th, the anniversary of the end of The Great War, later called World War One. Every year there were gigantic parades down Michigan Avenue in Chicago. There were rows and rows of men and women, several bands and hundreds of flags honoring veterans from America's wars. Most vets marched, many in military or American Legion uniforms, but I saw several Civil War Veterans riding in open cars. It was a great day. Little did we boys know what was in store for us in the future? Some day we would be the veterans of an even bigger war.

XI

These are some of the people I remember as a boy: My dad had a friend by the name of Ed Hunsaker. Ed, his wife Ethlyn and their daughter Louise, had come to Northbrook from Galesburg, Illinois. They were originally from Missouri and some local people thought of the family as Hillbillies. Mr. Hunsaker was known as "Doc". Their daughter Louise was very spoiled and suffered with asthma. Her asthma seemed to become extremely bad when she didn't get her way with her parents. The kids all thought she was a pill. Since there were very few neighbors in our small community and our families had become friends I was often in the company of Louise. A cousin of Louise's, Alden Lindgren, lived with the family and became one of the boys I palled around with. Alden was the only boy of our group I lost touch with as we grew older and don't know what happened to him.

The Hunsakers lived about a quarter mile up Huehl Road which was a gravel path that ran north from Dundee Road. Hunsakers referred to Dundee as the Hard Road. They were quite poor and were on relief. Huehl Road was less than a half mile east of where we lived. The road was named after the Huehl family, an old woman and her son who lived on the northwest corner of Huehl and Dundee. The son was subject to epilepsy spasms and a couple of times I saw him rolling around on the floor while in one of his "fits". Why I was in their house I can't remember.

When I was about 15 years old I heard my father and Doc talking about the depression and how many people had their homes repossessed by the banks. It was Doc's opinion that in the event of another depression in later years, the Federal Government would step in and either put a moratorium on mortgage payments of those in arrears, or make some other arrangements to keep people from losing their homes. At the time his opinion was considered extreme but during the financial downturn of 2008 the Federal Government did bail out some people who should never have been approved for a home loan in the first place. The people who kept their homes by being saved by the government were resented by home owners who were paying off their mortgages on time. Some were furious, but nothing was done for them.

About half mile west of our house, at the intersection of Sanders and Dundee Roads, a family named Reeb had a gas station and car repair business. Reebs had several kids and my brothers and I went to school with all of them. The North Northfield Church we attended was on the northeast corner opposite Reebs. Sanders Road north of Dundee was a gravel road with several houses and farms.

One I remember well was the home of Al and Vera Paulson. Mr. Paulson had a cutlery manufacturing business in Chicago. The company made butcher, boning and other knives used by butcher shops and other markets that sold meats. His business operation was a little different than most. He didn't sell the knives outright, he rented them. Then he exchanged the used knives with sharpened or new ones as part of his service. Paulson invited me and a couple other boys who attended the church on the corner to his factory. Kenneth Caldwell and I went to the plant three or four Saturdays where we each made a general-use knife. Knives were made from scratch by cutting the blank blade from a steel plate, shaping it, tempering the red hot metal in ice cold water and attaching a wooden handle with four rivets. I gave my knife to my mother.

But what I got out of the weekends at Paulson's was much more valuable than the knife, or even the experience of making it. I already knew for certain I wanted my own business some day and those couple weeks at Paulson's factory strengthened my resolve. My business could be manufacturing, maybe even knives, or something else I could sell. Self employment was always my goal since the time I was a kid catalog salesman for Montgomery Ward. I don't remember Al Paulson other than the knife business very much except that he was always very upbeat and positive even during those tough days. He used the word "Splendid" quite often. He must have been a good salesman.

Vera was an art teacher who thought I had some talent so I took a couple lessons at their home. But I wasn't interested. Both Mr. and Mrs. Paulson were quite religious and active in the little church.

XII

The North Northfield church had an interesting history. I learned the church was founded in the simple log cabin of Daniel and Mary Esther Stanger and Rev. Jacob Boas preached the first sermon there in 1837. Daniel Stanger had walked almost the entire distance from eastern Pennsylvania to be the first settler in the area. His reports encouraged more German-speaking settlers to follow him.

Until a few years before we moved to the area Sunday Services had been preached in German. After a few years they added a second service in English later in the morning. By the time we began attending church the services were all in English, although many people in and around Northbrook spoke both languages. Because of my earlier experiences with the German workers at Northbrook Gardens, I still spoke enough German to converse with some of the older people.

None of the other kids could do that and some of them thought I was also from Germany.

The church building was all wood with a huge bell tower. On Sunday mornings the tolling of the big bell could be heard for miles around. In depression Sundays, the roads were almost deserted, with few cars to muffle the bell's solemn tone. Before we ever attended services in the church I was a caddy at the University Golf Club. The green of the third hole was just a few yards from the church building. As I was standing, while holding the flag pole, waiting for the golfers to "hole out", I could hear the congregation singing. I thought it was a very pleasant, soothing sound.

When we became members in the mid 30s there was a row of several stalls behind the church. That was where people from earlier congregations had kept their horses on Sunday mornings. I don't remember when they were demolished.

Some years later we saw flames that seemed to be coming from the sky itself in the direction of the church. Somehow the old building had caught fire and burned to the ground. For some reason I still remember part of the interior although not what the building looked like outside. It was a building that might have been of historical value.

During that time I was also attending catechism classes. I remember asking the Pastor who it was that decided at the Council of Nicaea called by Emperor Constantine, which books would be included in the Bible. He said the decisions were made by men who were inspired by God. I told him I didn't believe that, but don't know why I was so skeptical

Our family home was bigger than most and the basement was frequently used for parties, with dancing to the music of a four or five piece "orchestra". The musicians usually consisted of a saxophone, maybe two, an accordion, guitar, and drums. I don't recall how talented they were, but I do remember one of the wives at the parties had a crush on the sax player that became a source of local gossip. And, most of all I remember that, although kids were generally excluded from the parties, Louise was there and she became the first girl I ever kissed, at least in a way that romance could be inferred from the kiss.

Nothing came of our relationship, but I did get a bit closer with her friend Edith, who lived at the corner of Dundee Road and Huehl Road. It was in a tent one afternoon. I was 14 and she was a year older. She and I took all her clothes off but she said she was afraid so nothing serious happened. Later I wondered why Edith's mother, who was only a few feet away in the kitchen, didn't suspect something was going on out there in the tent. Edith got married two three years later. Some of the girls I knew were married quite young. Edith married at about 17.

Edith's brother Ed's suicide was my first experience with death. My friend Teddy Marbet went with me to the Langfield farm home where the body was on display and we were both shocked at how still a dead person looked. I don't know how we expected him to appear, neither of us had ever seen a person in a casket before. Another Langfield son, Richard, committed suicide later and Edith's father Bill did the same thing by parking his model T Ford on the Milwaukee Railroad tracks in front of an on coming express train. He didn't know, or care, that Shotgun Louie, one of the local bootleggers, was passed out in the back seat when the locomotive hit the model T. Not long after the Langfield deaths Teddy's father died of Hepatitis, called Yellow Jaundice in those days. I felt very sorry for Teddy.

That track crossing Dundee Road was where I once sat wishing I could be aboard the train and was the scene of several bad accidents. I remember vividly one time my dad and I stopped right after a train had hit a car. To this day I can still see, in my "mind's eye", a man lying face down along the track, motionless, except he was moving one of his legs slightly. My dad tried but couldn't help him. He must have been thrown from the car and while we were there no one else came to his aid. It could have been too late for him and probably no one knew what to do to help. I never learned who he was. That would be of no interest to a kid I guess.

Until my grandfather, my mother's father, died when I was in my junior year in high school I didn't have any family experiences with death. Mildred Wright, a girl I went to grade school with, died one summer and Charles Palmer, my "body guard" drowned in the filthy Des Plaines River about the same time. But I wasn't with either at the time of their deaths. Charles hated his half brother Fritz who tried to bully me. So Charles became my bodyguard in school. The summer Charles died I grew about 2 or 3 inches and since Fritz was little fellow he never thought it wise to bully me again. I never felt revenge because I saw Charles' real father cry at the cemetery when Charles was buried.

Almost all the kids I grew up with became smokers. Had they not, I probably would have smoked cigarettes myself just to be different. I had no "horse sense" as a youngster. It was many years before I did learn to be more practical, in fact I became very good at using common sense in most business matters.

Sometime during 1934 I heard that the big Chicago mail order house, Montgomery Ward was looking for catalog salesmen. During the depression men applied for jobs they would never do at other times. This was one of those jobs. When I applied for the job by mail I neglected to tell Wards that I was only 12 years old. But, after awhile, it seemed to me an eternity, a Ward's sales kit arrived in the mail. My mother had a carrying case that was the right size to hold the big Wards catalog. I immediately began calling on people in the neighborhood and sold several, mostly small, items. One farmer, Mr. Schneider, who was the father of two of my school mates, Arthur and Raymond, ordered a fairly large amount of barbed wire. I didn't always take money for my sales commission. I often opted to take my commissions in merchandise. I selected several items and most of all I remember getting a 16 mm movie projector along with some black and white film. One of the films was a movie of old time actor Buck Jones. It was one of our favorite movies that my friend Billy Christman and I played in the darkness of his father's cold storage building. That was when we dreamed of some day making real movies in Hollywood with our company, H & C Movie Company.

During summer vacations my job cutting down the weeds in the peony and iris gardens kept me pretty busy. The iris plants were in short rows going north to south, unlike the peonies in much longer east to west rows. The iris field began a couple yards from Dundee Road, extending about 30 feet north to a grass path that led from our driveway to a rock garden. Dad had built the garden and a pool next to the cemetery parking lot. Bordering the back of the rock garden were tall evergreens that blocked the view of any of the few cars that might be in the cemetery parking lot. There were about 50 rows of iris, so I had quite a job keeping the weeds down. I used a long handled hoe that had to be sharpened frequently because the weeds were tough and the ground baked hard in the hot summer sun. I would sharpen the hoe in the garage with a big steel file.

I spent a lot of time while in the iris patch thinking about how I would go about owning my own business some day. I had just seen the Walt Disney movie "Snow White and the Seven Dwarfs". I didn't care too much for the movie itself, but was interested in cartoon films as a business. I learned as much as I could about Walt Disney and how Snow White has been produced and financed with many problems. Of course I knew my chances of going to Hollywood were somewhere between zero and zip, never the less I soon envisioned a movie studio full of my own cartoonists, perhaps right near the peony farm. My idea was to adapt the scripts I had already thought up for radio, to various cartoon characters. But, it turned out to be just another idea I had no way of putting into action, like the collapsible row boat I had recently built that I didn't know how to sell.

But, I did already know one fact of life at a very early age. That was no matter how good or practical my ideas might be, they had to be sold or the whole plan was worthless. In the mid 30s the Chrysler Corporation was making a car with a new radical design, the 1937 Chrysler "Airflow". They also made the DeSoto with the same Airflow features. I often visualized myself with a brand new DeSoto, coming home after a successful sales trip, selling some product I had manufactured.

My dad always claimed he disliked salesmen, but in reality he was the greatest salesman I ever knew. The peony farm itself meant little until the flowers and peony roots had been sold. Later, dad created sales for the nursery he established north of the peony fields.

By the worst of the Great Depression many of the people in Northbrook worked either for my dad or the Culligan Soft Water Company. Dad had crews of people working on his projects, but did all the selling himself. In those days most all parents did not discuss family business with their children, so I didn't know at that time, how or why our peony business really became successful. It was because of my father, Ray Hallen. He built it, and with the help of our mother Louise, made it successful and profitable during the worst of the Great Depression.

A couple of summers during the peony season my dad assigned me the evening job of selling bunches of peony flowers in front of Phil Johnson's, a busy restaurant on Waukegan Road. I liked that job and meeting people came naturally to me. I was never shy or nervous about meeting strangers. At the ages of 12 and 13 I had absolutely no fear of calling on people when making sales calls for Wards or selling flowers.

I liked the job at Phil Johnson's but when working in the garden cutting down weeds I spent more time watching airplanes from Sky Harbor flying directly overhead as they flew the pattern around the airport. They were student pilots and some days the wind was so strong from the southwest that the old Fledgling Airplanes almost stood still in the air. I knew nothing about how and why an airplane succeeded in flying and feared the plane would stall and crash. I don't know if my early fears had anything to do with my later enlistment in the Naval Air Corps in 1942, but am sure now my joining had more to do with avoiding being drafted into the Army.

XIII

There was a great deal of activity at Sky Harbor Airport even at the depth of the depression. The man who managed the airport and operated the flying school could often be seen, and especially heard, flying his Ryan low wing monoplane high over the airport in late afternoon, performing all sorts of aerobatics. I remember watching him more than once while standing in our back yard. The noise of the engine would catch my attention and I would look up and see the silver plane against the blue sky quite high above the airport. Sky Harbor was so close to our house it looked as though he was directly overhead. He would dive the plane straight down toward the ground and then, with the engine screaming, pull up doing barrel rolls as the plane gained altitude. We heard he was drunk during these maneuvers.

The end of Sky Harbor's north-south runway was just a few feet from Dundee Road. Planes landing would be quite low as they crossed Dundee just before touch down. One day my dad happened to be driving past the runway when a Piper Cub bounced very lightly off the top of his car. Dad said he just laughed and continued on his way home. When my cousin Bob from Belvedere would visit us with his father, my dad's brother Terry, Bob would insist on spending all the time he could at Sky Harbor. He became a B-24 Bomber pilot during the 2nd Word War.

During early summer of 1930 the four Hunter Brothers established a record for endurance flight, circling the area around Sky Harbor. Brothers John and Kenneth Hunter were in the Stinson SM-1 airplane with "The City of Chicago," painted on the fuselage. They were supported by in-flight refueling from another Stinson SM-1, flown by their brothers Albert and Walter. The record-setting endurance flight lasted from June 11 through July 4th.

I remember very clearly listing to the Stinson engine during the night between thunder claps from the summer storms. During the day we could watch them as they flew quite low and stayed close to the airport and our home. Huge crowds would gather around the Sky Harbor Club House as they few overhead.

One brother, Kenneth, even went outside the plane on a catwalk inspecting the engine while in flight. His picture was taken from the other airplane and widely circulated in newspapers all over the country. It was reported that this brother also opened up a door in the roof of the Stinson, and catching the long hose from the plane above, would put it into the wing tank and refuel the plane. I learned many years later the endurance plane used 18 gallons of gas an hour so the refueling had to be done often, even in the dark of night and during thunder storms. I also heard a report that Kenneth changed spark plugs while the engine was running and rebuilt a magneto. I doubted the story about the magneto. The brothers were finally forced to discontinue their flight due to oil filter failure and gasoline leak problems, but only after setting a new endurance record of 553 hours and 41minutes.

In these early development days of aviation, a spirit of sport and competition became a major aspect of its ever-growing appeal. Air races began to enjoy worldwide popularity. The most well known were the Cleveland Air Races where names like Roscoe Turner, Lowell Bayles and Jimmy Doolittle began to appear in newspapers as winners. Doolittle became famous again in 1942 when he led the B-25 Bomber Raid on Japan. His planes took off from an aircraft carrier.

My dad was an avid fan of general aviation from its very beginning and one of the first to fly in commercial aviation. My dad and I often attended the air races, sometimes taking my young brother Elmer as well.

One of the major races in our area was held at the Chicago Municipal Airport, later named Midway Airport. We kids didn't know the word municipal meant city and we mispronounced the word as "muni-sip-ull" airport. Air races were a lot of fun and very noisy.

My dad had a friend who established the altitude record in a non-oxygen equipped airplane. He flew so high the liquid in his eyes froze but did no permanent damage. Once dad and I went to Sky Harbor the day a man, whose name I remember for some reason was Able, attempted a world record for the number of loops he could do in a glider, starting at a pre-determined altitude. I don't remember the number of loops but he broke the record, although the last loop occurred so close to ground it looked like he wouldn't make it. At the end of the last loop the plane was back on the runway again. A close call but those men faced danger willingly and often.

Sometimes their pioneering ended in tragedy. Once, also at Sky Harbor, two men rebuilt a Curtis Robin airplane. I saw them working on it all during one summer. After long days of work the job was finally completed and the Robin ready for a test flight. On the Sunday afternoon when they did their trial flight the plane stalled, crashed and burned at the end of the runway with their wives and families watching. The tragedy happened just north of our peony garden. People rushed to the crash but the plane was on fire and the pilots had died. One man who came to the scene, Dick Langfield, tried to pull the gas tank from the fire but without success.

Names of the air race pilots and their planes were well known to me and my neighbor Teddy Marbet. Teddy was very skilled at building models of these planes out of balsa wood and paper. Models were powered by twisted rubber bands that turned the propeller. I tried making them too but was not very good at it.

Sky Harbor had a glider that held a single pilot. The "grease monkeys" who worked on the planes would tow the glider with its single occupant down the runway behind an old Chevy. When the glider was high enough it was cut loose and the pilot made a 180 degree turn and landed. Although by then I knew how airplanes flew, and washed planes and did other work for free flying lessons, I still didn't have enough experience to try flying the glider myself.

A couple boys and I did build a glider one time from parts of old airplanes we got from Sky Harbor. I was the instigator but had lots of encouragement and help. Almost all the planes at the airport, an exception being the Ford Tri-Motor and other larger planes, were made of wood, some aluminum and fabric. The fabric was usually linen stretched over the wings and fuselage. It was then sprayed with a liquid that tightened the fabric so it became hard, somewhat like the surface of a drum. Then it was painted. The fabric was subject to cuts and had to be patched occasionally. But when the fabric became old it was replaced. This discarded fabric is what we used to cover the wings of our glider. It had one seat.

Our idea was, like the glider at the airport, to tow it to get it airborne. We had plenty of open land for the car to run on and Billy Christman's father had an old Ford we could use. Since no one wanted to be the first "pilot" we decided to make sure it would fly. So with a lot of labor we finally got the thing up on the slopping roof of the Northbrook Gardens garage. We hooked up a rope and off we went. The glider came to the end of the building and fell straight down and crashed. It didn't even go forward an inch. The wing collapsed too. As fast as we could we got rid of the wreckage before Billy's dad found out what we had done to the garage roof, which was now missing some of its shingles.

Sky Harbor hosted air races every summer and one of the pylons that racers made turns around was on the farm directly across from our house. The planes flew very low as well as fast and we could see and hear them rounding the pylon with engines roaring at full throttle. Those days were an exciting time for the whole neighborhood, a relief from depression stress.

The period from the late 1920s to the mid-1930s was known as "The Golden Age of Air Racing." We were all part of that Age. National Air races were sponsored by well intentioned entrepreneurs, offering thousands of dollars in prize money. The Pulitzer Trophy Race was sponsored by an American newspaperman, Ralph Pulitzer, to promote high speed in landplanes. The Thompson Trophy Race in Cleveland was an All American spectacular event. Jimmy Doolittle won the Thompson Trophy in 1932 in a Gee Bee, although he usually flew a plane known as the Laird Super Solution.

The Pulitzer Trophy Race was won by Roscoe Turner in a plane called the Meteor, a plane he designed himself that was built by the Laird Company.

On the day of the Pulitzer Trophy Race, at ten o'clock in the morning, process servers came to the airport to seize Roscoe Turner's plane for debt. His mechanics kept the Meteor out of sight of the debt collectors. Turner flew the race and won it and had the money to pay off his debts. That is how aviation was financed in the 1930's. Teddy and I knew all the names of the pilots and planes. But there were fatal accidents too, although none in the Sky Harbor races.

The Gee Bee flown by Doolittle was an extremely dangerous airplane to fly, and several men and one woman were killed in them. Built by Granville Brothers from where it got its name, it was short and fat, basically a flying engine with wings. I have a video clip of Lowell Bayles killed in an out of control Gee Bee in 1931. The clip is difficult to watch as there are close up shots of the pilot before taking off.

Later, at 300 miles an hour, the plane, at very low altitude, barrel rolled into a fire ball crash. At first I heard the cause of the accident was because the gas cap had come off the tank right in front of the pilot and broke the windshield, hitting and incapacitating Bayles. Later digital examination of the film showed the actual cause was aileron flutter. The very short wings and tiny ailerons on the Gee Bee caused many of the fatal crashes.

The days of Gee Bee racing are over. That exciting part of my life was finished by the time I started high school. The Granville Brothers are gone. But replicas of the Gee Bee are still being flown. I have a spectacular video of a reproduction being flown, with aerobatics that are truly stunning. I wish I could have flown a Gee Bee myself.

The middle years of the depression were also the beginning of commercial passenger flight, and Grey Goose Airlines used Sky Harbor as their headquarters. I never flew in one of their planes, but another company provided scenic flights, charging for tickets by the weight of the passenger. The cost was a penny a pound. I went with my dad. He was well over 6 foot 2 and weighed nearly 200 pounds so he paid two bucks. I weighted 60 pounds so my ticket cost sixty cents. We flew in a very noisy Ford Tri Motor over the Lake Michigan shoreline and back. I thought it was a very short flight.

In the 1930s the men who flew these planes were pioneers who risked their lives in flimsy wood and canvas aircraft, with questionable power and poor controls. They often paid with their lives for the great age of aviation that followed. I feel honored to have been witness to that interesting period in America, and to eventually witness the day in 1969 when it all culminated with a man walking on the surface of the moon and returning safely to earth.

Gee Bee   My favorite airplane I never got to fly

Grove School 1931

Mom and Dad

Me and Elmer 1924

Me in 1926

With Granddaughters 2000

Northbrook Shermer avenue 1924

At Lauderdale Lake

Unemployed

President Roosevelt

1933 Fair Poster

Theatro de Lago

Elmer Hallen

Grove School Kids

Northbrook School 1938

Grove School Kids 1931

Our Home 1935   Glenbrook Gardens

Eleanora

WHY CAN'T YOU GIVE MY DAD A JOB?

Chicago Sttreet 1935

Chicago World's Fair 1933

Chicago Theater

Bread Line 1934

Cast of Dinner at Eight

Soap Opera Cast 1935

Soap Kitchen 1936

Very Popular

Author in 2012

Chicago Worlds Fair 1933
Avenue of The Flags

Tigers vs Cardinals
Worlds Series 1934

Kenneth Hunter in Flight 1930

John Held Jr. Flapper Drawing

Katzenjammer Kids Hans und Fritz

"Keep Walking" 1932

Sky Harbor Airport 1930

Wrigley Field

XIV

I remember much of the presidential campaign and election of 1932, which was run against the backdrop of the depression, because my dad had become interested in politics. Franklin Delano Roosevelt won the Democratic nomination and campaigned on a platform of attention to "the forgotten man" at the bottom of the economic pyramid. Hoover continued to insist it was not the government's job to address the growing economic and social crisis.

Dad was glad when Roosevelt won in a landslide. Roosevelt took office on March 4, 1933, with the declaration that "the only thing we have to fear is fear itself." I heard that speech myself on our Philco radio. My father was a great supporter of Roosevelt as were most of the people in Northbrook and even more so in the city of Chicago.

After prohibition was repealed in 1933, many taverns and bars located in Chicago had large photographs of the new President prominently displayed. In later years, long after the depression was over, I saw many of those same pictures still in their original place of honor, although smoke and time had diminished the image.

I also heard FDR's famous radio speech in which he said the American people needed "A New Deal" The term New Deal came to known as a political phrase referring to

Roosevelt's entire program for ending the depression. His distracters used the term in a derogatory way. The new President also offered, and Congress passed, a series of emergency measures that came to characterize his promise of that new deal for the American people.

But Roosevelt's efforts to assert government control over the economy were frustrated by Supreme Court rulings that overturned key pieces of legislation. As a 12 year old I knew much of this because but my dad followed the news every day in the papers and on radio, and we talked about what was happening.

During the winter of 1933-34 my dad worked for the National Park Service during the winter months when the peony roots were frozen in the ground. Roosevelt had created a temporary job program named The Civilian Conservation Corps. Dad supervised the work done by the CCC enrollees who were mostly young men, most of whom came from the bigger cities in the east. They had joined the CCC to support themselves and their families while learning new trades and skills. Dad gained great respect for the program and its effect on young men. Most had never been out of the city and their work in the national parks, many in states like Idaho and California, was beneficial to themselves and the country.

Winters in Illinois sometimes brought temperatures that caused rain to turn to ice as it fell. We kids would ice skate on the roads that had become covered with ice. One Saturday I skated to my dad's Park Service office which was about 2 or 3 miles distant. Two others boys went with me. Getting there on the ice was great fun, but my dad was gone, so we had no ride home. Now the sun was out, the ice melted rapidly and we had brought no shoes. There was no way we could have called home for help so we suffered the torture of walking alternately with our shoe skates on, then in our stocking feet.

My father held the CCC in such good regard that he enlisted me as an enrollee in 1940. But by then the program had deteriorated and was abandoned shortly after. But I did see a couple CCC boys some years later on a troop train while I was in the Navy. CCC uniforms looked very much like those worn by soldiers in the First World War.

Another program my dad admired for the work it accomplished was the Civil Works Administration. The CWA employed more than four million men and women at jobs from building and repairing roads and bridges, parks, playgrounds and public buildings to creating art.

The Federal Writers Project gave many writers their first opportunity to have their works published. There was an excellent history of each of the 48 States produced by the FWP. I did not see the one for Illinois where we lived but many years later when I was publishing a travel magazine named Scenic Idaho Magazine, I was able to obtain a well worn copy of the Writers Project Book for Idaho that was very valuable when researching the history of the Gem State. Copies of the Idaho book are very rare because Idaho had little population and few books were printed. My copy was stolen from me by a dishonest bookseller named Sam Weller in Salt Lake City.

When I was the Navy, stationed briefly in Pocatello, Idaho in 1943, the green wooden city ball park had been built by CWA workers. Another government program was the WPA that employed more unskilled workers cleaning parks, ditches and roads.

Not all people were Roosevelt supporters. When I was in my second year in high school one of the teachers complained vociferously about Roosevelt and his "make-work" programs. He did this while several student's fathers were out in the school yard cleaning up the property. No one said anything. Maybe the kids didn't pay any attention to what the teacher said. I noticed the irony because at even an early age ironic situations intrigued me.

In 1936 the Republican Party nominated the Governor of Kansas, Alfred M. Landon as their presidential candidate to run against Roosevelt. Landon was a successful oil man and lawyer before he became Governor and the Republican Party believed him to be a strong candidate. I remember Landon had very few in supporters in Cook County, the county that included Northbrook. The ones who wanted him to win wore gigantic buttons with a sunflower in the middle.

Roosevelt won in a landslide again. A nationally circulated magazine, The Literary Digest, became infamous for predicting a Landon victory. My dad subscribed to the Digest and liked their articles even though the publication was co-founded by Robert McCormick, publisher of the Chicago Tribune, whom he did not like. My dad was very liberal in the sense that he believed everyone had a right to their personal opinions even if different than his. He respected other people's point of view.

Even after Roosevelt's big victory in 1936, Congress rejected much of the New Deal proposals. The Supreme Court overturned others, but not before the Social Security Act creating old-age pensions went into effect. Dad was a great supporter of Social Security. I was too in later years when I knew more about its purpose. I am distressed now when the savings we put into Social Security are discounted and the program considered a government benefit, in other words, free stuff.

XV

On very hot summer days when the temperature was in the high 90's, and very humid, we would leave the field work and spend the afternoon indoors listening to the Cubs baseball games on WGN Radio. In 1937 I felt as though I knew the players personally, Augie Galan in left field, Ki Ki Kyler in center, Frank Demere right field, Stan Hack at third, Billy Jurgus short stop, Billy Herman at second and of course Charlie Grim, manager and first baseman. Grimm later became full time manager and Phil Cavoretta took over at first. In his initial appearance in a Cub uniform at Wrigley Field 18 year old Cavoretta hit a home run that won the game over Cincinnati. Gabby Hartnett was the main catcher and I remember only two pitchers, Lon Warneke and Bill Lee. Warneke was later an umpire. I often visualized myself as one of the players when listening to those games.

Cubs games at Wrigley Field started at 3 in the afternoon. The reason was to give Chicago businessmen time to get to the games after most of the day was spent in the office. Very few women attended ball games in the thirties and the men were almost always dressed in suits with shirts and ties.

Street cars and the "L" stopped right at Wrigley Field's gates. Cubs Park, as it was often called, is still located in a residential area. Local kids would wait behind the ball park on Waveland Avenue, hoping to catch home run balls hit out of the park. I wanted to go back there too but my dad said no.

There was no parking lot at the ball park, so when we went to the games we parked, like most others, on side streets and in alleys. Some people rented space in their drive ways and even in their yards. I thought that was part of going to the game, locating a place to park and remembering after the game where we left our car. There were some big apartment buildings on the street behind the bleachers where people who lived in them would sit on the roofs and watch the games.

All games in those days were played during the day. I heard my dad tell a friend that the Cubs owner, William Wrigley, Junior, hated night baseball and felt the game should be played only in summer and only during the day. Many, many years later Wrigley Field did put in lights. I never went to a night game in that ball park. When I see pictures of the front of Wrigley Field today I immediately let my mind wander and I'm back in that wonderful time, just for a few moments.

The other Chicago baseball team was The White Sox who played their games in Comiskey Park on the South Side. The White Sox were in the American League. The Cubs were a National League Team. I never attended a baseball game at Comiskey Park but one cold winter day saw a football game there between the Chicago Cardinals and The Pittsburg Steelers. The seats we sat on were made of concrete and extremely cold. My two uncles were White Sox Fans although both lived on the north side of Chicago. Some people called the team "The Black Sox" because of an old scandal in the early 1900s when some players were accused of "throwing the game." I never knew any of the details and didn't care. The Cubs were my team.

In 1937 dad started another business in addition to the peony farm. It was the business of landscaping homes and estates on the Lake Michigan North Shore and in the Northbrook-Glenview areas. Dad began to hire men who had formerly been unemployed or were ex-WPA workers. I also worked with these landscaping crews during spring vacation and summers when I wasn't working at Sportsman's Golf Course. Some of the new business projects required extensive design and considerable time to complete, since the work had to stop during winter months. Dad did most of the design work, although he did employ some landscape architects as well.

Another new company had also started business in Northbrook, It was the Culligan Zeolite Soft Water Company and soon many of the men who had jobs in Northbrook were employed either by my dad or Culligan.

The Culligan story is an interesting one. During the boom era of the 1920s, several new subdivisions were built in and around Northbrook. Streets, sewers, lights and utilities were installed, but the depression stopped the construction of homes to populate the subdivisions. The streets were empty, just a couple houses spotted here and there in the vast complexes. We kids would ride our bikes up and down the empty streets. After dark, most of the scattered houses in the neighborhood were uninhabited and dark. I heard many people say the whole project would be abandoned.

With the coming of the war in 1942 some houses were sold, but no more built until after the war. The Zeolite used by Culligan needed to be spread out and dried before being put into canisters for use by consumers. The empty streets in Northbrook's partly finished subdivisions were ideal for the drying process. So the company paid a fee to the city for use of the streets and that effectively ended our bicycle riding on those streets.

XVI

Sometime in the 1920s, well before the Depression, my grandparents, my mother's father and mother, bought a summer home at Lauderdale Lakes in southern Wisconsin. That part of the Badger State contains many various size lakes, the most notable is Lake Geneva. Lauderdale and Geneva are close to the town of Elkhorn, once the hunting and camping grounds of the Pottawatomi and Algonquian Tribes. As a family, and with friends, we often spent summer vacations at Lauderdale. My grandfather stayed at the place most of each summer after he retired.

The house was a single story frame building built on a rather steep hill. Under the front of the house, facing the lake, was a storage space where boats and other items were kept. A gravel path ran from the back door, alongside the building, down hill to the dock. A couple of flat bottom boats were attached to the side of the dock. Both were painted green.

Once when I was about 9 or 10 I fell off the end of that dock and was pulled out of the water sputtering and coughing by my uncle John.

The drive from Northbrook to Lauderdale Lakes was less than 90 miles. My brother Elmer and I, neither had ever been anywhere outside Northbrook, would have dad stop the car (there was almost to traffic) at the State Line and we would solemnly walk from Illinois to Wisconsin. Southern Wisconsin was very rural. I remember that in spring the dirt roads throughout that part of the state were lined with long deep ruts in the mud that made travel very difficult. More than one driver slid off the road and had to be pulled out by horses furnished by local farmers.

Once we got to the lake area the narrow roads were at least graveled. One road led to the small parking lot at the top of a hill with a path leading down to the house. A neighbor, Sven Larsen, had to back his Model T up the hill to the parking lot. The road was too steep for his car to navigate forward. I never knew the reason his particular Ford had to do that.

At the corner of the road leading up the hill was a grocery and general store named Konke's. They seem to supply most or all of the needs of homes on that side of Middle Lake, the one of the four lakes where our place was located. Konke's could also be accessed from the lake. It was about a 10 minute row from our dock to Konke's Store.

On the way to Konke's by boat it was possible to see a gigantic rock that looked to be about 3 or 4 feet under water. The water in all the lakes was very clear. One day my uncle John decided to get out of the boat and stand on the rock. He got out but went down over his head because the water had distorted the rock's depth that was actually more like 10 feet down, not 3 or 4.

The daily mail was delivered by motor boat. Our dock, like the others I saw, had a mail box at the end. As I mentioned, we were on what was called Middle Lake the smallest of the 3 that had deep water. Another lake named Mill began at about Konke's Store. It was located in the opposite direction from Middle, but the water was so low the lake was more of a swamp and not useable. It consisted of shallow water, overgrown with cat tails and other vegetation.

There are many small islands in the lakes, plus plenty of open water so there was unlimited opportunities for boating, fishing, and other outdoor activities. The largest was Green Lake, located to the left of our lake. Green Lake seemed to be where the more wealthy homes were located. Some of the houses were very big. There was also a summer resort there and more speedboats. Most boats were bigger and seemed to be faster. There was a great deal of surf boarding, sometimes with two people being towed behind a boat. I never saw any water skiing. My brother and I rowed over into Green Lake once but got so tired going back we never went there again.

Like many of the lakes in Wisconsin, the Lauderdale Lakes are glacier formed. As glaciers slowly moved through the area they left behind thousands of lakes and springs. Middle and Mill Lakes are characterized by being called drainage lakes, fed primarily by groundwater, precipitation and runoff. All the water in the three lakes flows through Mill Lake to an outflow located on the eastern shore and into Honey Creek. A dam built on that creek in the mid 1800s helped raise water levels and continues to maintain the level of the lakes. Green Lake is the only spring-fed one.

I remember the torrential rains we had each summer, so heavy we could often see the water level in Middle Lake had risen quite a bit during the rainfall. The lake around the shoreline was a little muddy but we did swim a couple times off the end of the dock.

We had a big net on the dock for catching minnows we used for bait. We did a lot of fishing for blue gills and sun fish which were plentiful.

From the front porch, or from the dock, it seemed to us kids like a long way across the water to the houses and docks on the other side. We didn't think anyone could swim that far.

But many years later, in 1971, when I stopped to see the old place, I was surprised to see it was actually a fairly short swim had anyone done it.

XVII

In one of those strange paradoxes that frequently occur in history, The Great Depression of the 1930s also brought with it the "Golden Age of Radio". Radio was one of the few bright spots during the Hard Times years. The primary source of home entertainment for the general public during the thirties was radio. That is where much of the news came from as well.

Although the first radio I remember was a battery operated one over which we heard the news of Lindbergh's landing in Paris, by the 1930s radio networks were already linking their stations to the major broadcasting centers of New York City and Chicago. William Paley had organized the Columbia Broadcasting System, a wide ranging radio network. Others were NBC, both Blue and Red networks and the Mutual Broadcasting System.

Radio was also well established as an advertising medium, selling products and services during the 20s, well before the Depression. And radio continued to sell during the worst of times. Listeners were entertained and the advertiser paid the bill.

Several national advertising agencies were already in business before 1930. By the time I was 11 or 12 years old I knew sponsors of my favorite programs had ad agencies who wrote the commercials. In fact I was well aware that one of the biggest ad agencies in the country, Lord & Thomas, was located in the Wrigley Building in Chicago. The owner of Lord and Thomas was Albert Lasker who started with the firm as a salesman. He was so good at obtaining clients he was soon made partner and eventually owned the agency. As a young boy I remember reading in the Chicago Tribune about the success of Albert Lasker, "Owner of the big Chicago Advertising Agency Lord and Thomas". He was famous for well known clients like Lucky Strike cigarettes and Quaker Oaks, as well as many other national advertisers. He was also well known for paying his copywriter, the famous Claude Hopkins, a fabulous salary while skimping on the pay of his other employees and making himself extremely wealthy.

As a copywriter Hopkins became famous as the originator of most advertising techniques used to day, like "Money back Guarantee" and using prominent people in product testimonials. His sales strategies changed national advertising more than any copywriter in the history of advertising.

Lasker was widely known for his ability to make millions of dollars every year and living in a fine estate in the midst of depression poverty. During the Great Depression's worst days Lasker was quoted as saying, "When the mob gathers in front of my estate and cries, 'Let's get the SOB that owns this place', I want to be in that crowd".

I once read a Lasker biography, "Taken at The Flood" by John Gunther. He was a great ad man but apparently not very likeable. Lasker retired in 1942 and his ad agency's name was changed to Foote, Cone, Belding and from then on managed and owned by men who had been branch managers of offices outside Chicago. I once I dated a girl who worked for FCB at the time of the agency's greatest years. The agency's headquarters were the in the Palmolive Building on Michigan Avenue. Michigan Avenue is as prominent in Chicago as Madison Avenue is in New York.

My personal agency idol was Leo Burnett, who started his ad agency in Chicago in 1935, right in the middle of the Great Depression. Because some men were selling apples on Chicago streets in 1935 when he went in business, Leo always had a bowl of apples on the front desk of each of his company offices.

The radio programs we listened to were often musicals, sponsored by companies whose names were included in the program title. Some were: The A&P Gypsies with conductor Harry Horlick, The Ipana Troubadours, a dance band directed by Sam Lanin. The Goodrich Zippers and The Cliquot Club Eskimos were others. The list was endless: Others were the Silvertown Cord Orchestra, featuring the Silver Masked Tenor, The Sylvania Foresters and The Flit Soldiers, all offering much the same musical style.

Prominent announces I remember were Phillips Carlin, John S. Young, Alwyn Bach and Charles Lyon. Lyon was the announcer on many programs that originated in Chicago and a sort of local celebrity.

Radio broadcast important news too I remember several reports of Charles Lindberg's historic flight over the Atlantic and landing in Paris, France in 1927. And later I heard FDR's famous speeches as he tried to end the depression.

Just before the stock market crash in 1929, a singer named Rudy Vallee had organized eight musicians and called them The Connecticut Yankees. Broadcasting a series of remote programs over WABC from New York's Heigh Ho Club, Vallee's trade mark introduction "Heigh Ho Everybody" was picked up and used by his listeners. He and his musicians had a knack for putting fun into their playing. And Rudy knew instinctively which songs were right for his musical style and with lyrics the audience would remember. One of his most popular songs was his theme song. My mother often played that song, "Your time is my time" on the piano in our home. She was an excellent pianist.

In 1932, the Rudy Vallee program began featuring guest stars, a new idea at the time. His Fleischmann's Yeast Hour became radio's first really big time variety program and set the pattern for every one that would follow. We listened to these programs and others on the Philco table top radio.

I saw Rudy Vallee one day in a Hollywood restaurant. I was in California attending a convention and don't remember the name of the place, but the people who took me there said it was well known. The floor was covered with sawdust. Although Rudy was long retired by then everyone in the place knew him. I was struck by his very curly hair.

My brother Elmer and I had crystal set radios that didn't require battery or electric power. They ran on the power received from radio waves through a long wire antenna. We would attach the antenna wire to a curtain rod atop one of the windows. A thin wire called a "cat whisker" could be moved to different spots on a piece of crystal to tune into various stations. The crystal was a small piece of mineral, generally galena.

Headphones, then called earphones, were the only listening devices. The signal was weak and only stations in Chicago could be picked up, but we could listen to Jack Armstrong, The all American Boy, Cubs baseball and a few more programs. That was good enough for us, although I remember our dad disliked Jack Armstrong intensely. I never learned why he hated that program, although he never stopped us from listening.

Other programs we listened regularly to as a family were comedy shows. Eddie Cantor on Sunday nights, sponsored by Chase and Sanborn Coffee, was very popular nationally although I didn't even want to listen to the program. I thought his so-called jokes about his several daughters were boring. Cantor insisted on a live studio audience, probably a first in radio broadcasting. He felt the sound of laughter would be contagious over the air. Actually, a person could almost feel the audience when they were laughing. It was much different than the canned laughter dubbed into comedy programs on television today.

Cantor also originated the idea of integrating his announcer into service as a straight man. I thought the announcer, Jimmy Wallington, was funnier than Cantor. Another Cantor announcer was Harry Von Zell, who was also with Fred Allen.

One of the most listened to comedians of the day was Ed Wynn, billed as the "Perfect Fool". I read one time in "Radio Stars", a popular magazine devoted to stories about radio personalities, that Wynn began his first time on the air by riding on the stage of the New Amsterdam Theatre on a small fire engine and started broadcasting as his sponsor Texaco's Fire Chief.

I really disliked Jack Pearl, known to his audience in 1933-34 as Baron Munchausen. Pearl was famous for his stories of outrages experiences no one believed really happened. When his announcer, originally played by Cliff Hall, doubted the truth of his tales the Baron would say, Vus you dare Sharley? It was his radio trade mark. Pearl's actual time at our house was relatively short. As far as I was concerned it was not short enough.

The real zany of the Depression-era was Joe Penner who became a national craze during the early 30s. I thought Penner's jokes were foolish and that he did the same routine too many times. I saw him in a bit part in a movie once. All I remember was he wore a small silly cap.

My whole family really enjoyed the Bob Hope program and we used his sponsor's Pepsodent tooth paste. The Jack Benny Program began with a male quartet spelling out the letters J-E-L-L-O.

In winter while listening to Jack Benny and his jokes about the palm trees and freeways of Southern California I could look out the window of our Northern Illinois home in zero weather and see snow skittering across the frozen lawn. I thought California, especially Hollywood, must be a very nice place to live. But never thought I would ever be a resident in the Golden Bear state.

By far, my personal favorite comedy program was The Fred Allen Show. His topical, sometimes caustic, humor was perfectly suited to my own taste and temperament. But I was bored with his running "feud" with Jack Benny and how they traded insults on each other's show. The only jokes from the feud I remember were when Allen described Benny, "He's a sour-puss. He's so mean he wouldn't give a toothpick to a starving woodpecker". Another was, "many times I've seen him with a razor blade, splitting a caraway seed between two canaries". One time he said he was going to hit Benny so hard on top of the head that when he woke up he would think he was in jail because he would be looking through his shoe laces. I didn't think any of that so called humor was funny.

But his characters on "Allen's Alley" were great. Allen's wife Portland Hoffa, in her innocent-sounding 13-year-old-girl voice, would ask Allen what question he was going to put to the Alley Citizens that night. Portland was an important asset to the show. Her stories of her mother were often a bright spot in the program. But I learned many years later that one sponsor, unknown to me, hated her and wanted Portland off the program. Fred Allen finally threatened to cancel the show if she had to be dropped and the sponsor backed down.

Some early characters on the Fred Allen program didn't last long. Among those were: Sarcastic, self-centered Senator Bloat, town drunk Sampson Souse and dimwitted Socrates

Mulligan. Each lasted only a few weeks. I was glad to see them replaced with people more to my taste. I liked pompous poet Falstaff Openshaw, played by Alan Reed, but my special favorites were Jewish housewife Pansy Nussbaum who always greeted Allen by saying, "You were expecting maybe...", and then she would mispronounce the name of a glamorous film star. "You were expecting maybe Tallulah Bunker?" (Tallulah Bankhead). Parker Fennelly was stoic New England farmer Titus Moody. Moody opened with: "Howdy, Bub". Once Moody told Allen, when asked how he was, "I'm mad today because I lost muh head" "How did that happen?" Allen asked. "I was in the yard drinking beer when a gust of wind come along and I lost muh head". Fennelly later became the television spokesman for Pepperidge Farms Products.

Kenny Delmar, the show's announcer, was also bellowing Southern Senator Beauregard Claghorn. His catch-phrases, "Somebody, Ah say, somebody knocked", "I'm from the South, Suh"; "That's a joke, son"; and "Pay attention, boy!" were repeated often by a couple of my friends in Grove School. Falstaff Openshaw's "That is precisely why I am here" was popular too.

Although I didn't know anything about the Fred Allen program's production in those days, I learned years later that, unlike Benny, Hope and others who employed joke writers, Fred Allen wrote the entire show himself. He worked 12 hour days, six days a week. His programs were broadcast Sunday nights. The show also featured The DeMarco Sisters, five vivacious young women who opened the program with a singsong "Mister Allen" repeated three times. Allen's rejoinder would be a witty line like. "It isn't Ma Perkins folks."

I once read a biographical book Fred Allen wrote, "Treadmill to Oblivion". In the book Allen described what it was like working with the radio networks during the 1930s. He said it was a highly competitive business and described how sponsors could affect program content. Allen had a running feud with censors too. I listened every week and couldn't understand any reason for censor's complaints.

Fred Allen was a stage name. His real name was John F. Sullivan and he was a staunch Catholic. His program often changed sponsors during its run, beginning with Tender Leaf Tea and Blue Bonnet Margarine.

By 12 years of age I had already become interested in the advertisers who sponsored the programs. I listened intently to the commercials, especially the singing jingles. Advertisers used sex, celebrities and pseudo science to sell, and they used newspapers, mass circulation magazines and the ubiquitous, and new in the1920's, radio to make their products national. In 1919 total advertising in the United States was estimated at 690,940 million and by 1929 the amount was the 3 billion per year. This inspired a great deal of buying, much of it on credit.

One of the more "grown up" programs that were popular was Easy Aces. Written by Goodman Ace and starring his wife Jane and her friend Marge, I never missed an episode if I could help it. Jane mispronounced words and used clichés in completely the wrong way. I thought the dialog was superb and it fascinated me and stirred my imagination, but I still don't know why it did. I guess I just liked offbeat humor.

I learned the cast sat around a card table when broadcasting because Ace felt the homey feeling the actors had would resonate to the radio audience.

When listening to re-runs of the shows, which of course were originally done live, I have tried to relate the jokes to depression times. Of course they were corny and never had a double meaning like so much humor today. During the depression of the 1930s the county had a much smaller population, more like a big family suffering hard times together, as I said before. And the audience makeup was far different. Hope, Benny, Canter, Allen and the others would not be particularly funny today in an ethnically diverse America.

Comedy wasn't all we listened to. Other nights many variety programs were available too, such as the very popular Bing Crosby Hour. At the end of each Crosby broadcast the announcer would say that the preceding program had been an electrical transcription. At the time I didn't know what that meant, but when I found out the show had been pre-recorded I never listened to Bing Crosby's program again. I wanted live entertainment. No one had any way of knowing that some day, with the invention of audio and video tape, almost all broadcasted programs radio and television, would be recorded in advance.

For much of the depression The National Barn Dance was a Midwest Craze. The program had debuted on WLS Radio on

April 19,1924, the first Saturday night after WLS signed on the air. After the first night's show had been going on about an hour, the station received over 25 telegrams of enthusiastic approval. But the management at Sears-Roebuck, owner of the station, did not like the "disgraceful low-brow music" that was being broadcast on their new station.

Although neither my parents or brothers cared much for The Barn Dance, I listened to Gene Autry, Eddie Dean, Lulu Belle and Scotty, and Pat Buttram on my crystal set radio every Saturday night. My favorites were the Hoosier Hot Shots, a quartette of zany players of banjos and a variety of drums, bells and whistles. I also liked Eddie Peabody playing the banjo. The Barn Dance announcer was Joe Kelly, later the host and moderator of NBC's Quiz Kids.

George Gobel was an Army Air Corps bomber instructor during WW-2 and became popular after the war as a comedian. Gobel was known on the Barn Dance as Little Georgie Gobel. He played the ukulele and sang.

In addition to the radio broadcasts, WLS performers also appeared in theaters, auditoriums and local fairs throughout Illinois, Wisconsin, Indiana, Michigan and Iowa. They would often be featured in local radio and newspaper advertising and were as recognizable to Chicagoans as movie stars, and just as popular.

There was a great deal of amateur theatrical production during the Depression years too. Many schools and clubs, such as The Elks and Masons, as well as churches, had stages in their facilities. The WLS Barn Dance was the inspiration for several amateur productions. Men and women would imitate the radio personalities and dress and perform as much like them as they could. Lulu Belle and Scotty and the Arkansas Wood Chopper were two of the many Barn Dance stars imitated by the amateurs.

My mother and dad appeared in some local stage productions too. Once mom was cast as a Russian Bolshevik woman who carried a bomb with the fuse lit around the stage and dad, who was a handsome man, played the part of a wealthy ladies man.

Known as The Smith Family on the Barn Dance, the husband and wife team of Jim and Marian Jordan left WLS for competitor station WMAQ and gained national notoriety as "Fibber McGee & Molly", which aired over NBC Network. Fibber and Molly became so popular that once during the summer I was walking down the street near my grandparent's home and heard the entire half hour program from the radios on the front porches as I passed by.

Another WLS program that was very popular was The Maxwell House Show Boat, a Depression-era version of wishing for the "cotton blossoms and magnolia days" of the Old South. I guess it was supposed to be an hour's relief from Depression woes. My parents listened to the program but to me the show's fictional Captain Henry and blackface deckhands Molasses and January were boring.

Dramatic radio programs were of secondary importance to my family during the depression years but not to me. Perhaps the first important full-scale drama to come out of Chicago was a weekly series for the Great Northern Railroad called "Empire Builders." This series offered half-hour tales set on the Empire Builder, The Great Northern crack train on the Chicago-Seattle run. With its sound effects and good acting by Don Ameche and Bernadine Flynn, I tried never to miss the program. Flynn was also Sade on my favorite daytime program Vic & Sade.

Other dramas of the depression we listened to were the True Story Hour and The First Nighter, both were favorites of my mother. Sherlock Holmes started in 1930, and Dr. Fu Manchu came later. There were many police and detective programs, often dramatizing events from real life. My grandmother, who lived with us after my grandfather died, loved all the crime shows. The more gruesome the story the better for her. My grandfather's all time favorite had been The Lone Ranger.

I avoided those programs but listened every day, when I was supposed to be doing my homework, to the kids programs like "Jack Armstrong, the All American Boy". That was the program my dad hated although he didn't stop me from listening and never told me the reason for his dislike. But I thought the boys in the show were engaged in adventures I would like to experience some day myself. The show was sponsored by Wheaties Cereal and opened with a singing jingle. "Wave the flag for Hudson High Boys, show them how we stand," was the start of it. Maybe it was the jingle dad disliked.

Most kid's shows were broadcast after school hours and were dramatized versions of popular cartoon characters. One of the earliest I remember was "Little Orphan Annie". Annie was a long-running strip in the Chicago Tribune. Although my family subscribed to the Herald-American every day we also got both the "Trib" and Herald on Sundays. To this day I remember a few of the opening lines of the title song. The rest I found "On Line":

Who's that little chatter box?
The one with pretty auburn locks?
Whom do you see?
It's Little Orphan Annie.
She and Sandy make a pair,
They never seem to have a care!
Cute little she,
It's Little Orphan Annie.
Bright eyes cheeks a healthy glow,
There's a store of healthiness handy.
Mite-size, always on the go,
If you want to know - "Arf", goes Sandy.
Always wears a sunny smile,
Now, wouldn't it be worth a while,
If you could be,
Like Little Orphan Annie?

Ovaltine was the show's longtime sponsor. I remember very well the secret decoders, rings, and shake-up mugs offered to members of the Little Orphan Annie Secret Society. The premiums were an integral part of the show.

Annie was Chicago actress Shirley Bell Cole. Beginning when she was ten years old she played Annie from 1930 to 1940. She died in 2011. I think this show is essential to any study of old time radio, and the production was often excellent. I was particularly interested in the program after I learned the scripts were written by various copywriters at Ovaltine's advertising agency. As Annie would say "Leapin' Lizards,"

Another program character adapted from the comics was Skeezix from Gasoline Alley. The show continued well into the war years of the 1940s. I didn't care for Skeezix and thought his Uncle Walt was just plain dumb.

Beside the kid's shows, I listened to dramatic programs like The Shadow, "What evil lurks in the mind of man? The Shadow knows" was part of the opening of the program.

Another of my favorites was One Man's Family. I thought the people were living fascinating lives, probably because I considered mine to be rather boring. I never went to China and India like the program's characters did.

The Chevrolet Chronicles was another radio show I avoided. The centerpiece of each program was an interview with a World War Medal of Honor winner, conducted by flying ace Eddie Rickenbacker. Despite my personal lack of interest I heard the show was popular, especially among people who lived through the First World War, originally called The Great War.

Of the many Ballrooms in Chicago the two I remember most of all, because of listening to their remote broadcasts, were the Aragon on the North Side and the Trianon at Cottage Grove and East 62nd Street on the South Side. The Trianon featured the music of Lawrence Welk who later became famous on television.

The Aragon was on West Lawrence Avenue in an area called Uptown. The Dick Jurgens Band with featured singer Eddy Howard played at the Aragon and were heard on hour long broadcasts from WGN Radio. I only went to the Aragon Ballroom once, long after its glory days. It was a huge room designed like a Moorish Palace. During the mid-30s they had over 18,000 people attend each week. Eddie Howard went on to become a featured singer on his own with several popular records to his credit. I only saw pictures of the Trianon, never went there.

Some very popular radio programs I remember were live broadcasts from the Marathon Dance Contests. Marathon Dances drew huge crowds and people followed their favorites faithfully. My dad thought the Marathons were foolishness but I don't know what my mother thought of them.

Dancers would push themselves to the limit for small prizes. They all started out as man and woman couples but if one fell asleep or dropped out for some other reason the other continued as a solo. The solo may join with another solo of the opposite sex and often did. Then they would have someone to hang onto when they were sleepy. I never went to one of the Marathons and am quite sure my parents did not go either. The pictures in the papers were not very pretty with each dancer looking like they were going to collapse any second. People all around us knew most of the dancer by name and Marathon Dancers were the subject of many conversations.

The Major Bowes Amateur Hour was broadcast nationally on Network Radio and was very popular with a wide audience. Some of the more talented contestants later became famous in radio, television and movies.

One was ventriloquist Paul Winchell, who, with his sidekick dummies Jerry Mahoney and Knucklehead Smiff, had one of the most watched television programs in the 1950s. Some years later Paul and I became friends in California. I began writing a biography of his interesting life, but unfortunately the book was never finished. Paul died before he could dictate enough for a complete story.

Paul Winchell was a very complicated but highly talented man, with several inventions and television innovations to his credit. Most notable was his development of an artificial heart. I have always been sorry his complete story was never told.

One of the older boys I went to high school with also appeared on the Bowes program. I only remember his first name was Ralph. He was a popular local saxophone player. Ralph, like Paul Winchell, was chosen to tour with one of the Bowes Groups who made personal appearances. Ralph was soon kicked off the group for appearing while drunk.

One of the most popular radio programs of all time, and I never missed it, was Amos and Andy. Two white actors who portrayed an entire cast of colored characters. The cast consisted of Amos, a cab driver, Andy, a not too bright patsy and The Kingfish, a con man who was always trying to trick Andy out of his money. Kingfish was played by Amos.

Amos 'n' Andy wasn't just a radio program, especially during 1930-31, it was an obsession. This simple little fifteen minute serial gripped the attention of as many as forty million listeners six nights a week. The program was so popular I remember more than once going to see a movie and having the movie interrupted so the audience could listen to Amos & Andy. The movie would resume at the end of the radio program.

The most popular daytime radio programs during the mid 30s were the short 15 minute episodes that became known as "Soap Operas" because so many were sponsored by soap companies. When I was about 12 or 13 I often thought of some day writing scripts for these programs. I even developed a group of characters, and often when working in the yard, would develop what I thought was a plot. I didn't know how to contact anyone in that business but I wrote out several ideas for my imaginary characters.

At 12 years of age I didn't know any of the connections between the radio stations and the ad agencies that produced the programs. I did know that almost all the soap opera programs were written and produced live in Chicago, just a few miles away from our home. Most originated in radio station studios in the Merchandise Mart, in 1930 the largest building in the country.

My favorite soap, Vic & Sade was broadcast at 12:30, during the school lunch period. Since we lived next door to Grove School I would scurry home, eat quickly and enjoy the 15 minute program. Vic and Sade was the most popular radio series of its kind and reported by Time Magazine to have reached more than seven million listeners. It ran for fourteen years and for the majority of its time on the air Vic and Sade was heard in 15-minute episodes without a continuing storyline. I enjoyed every episode and soon identified with the central characters, known as "radio's home folks". They were accountant Victor Rodney Gook, his wife Sade and their adopted son Rush. The three lived on Virginia Avenue in what the announcer called "the small house half-way up in the next block". The program was done with low-key ease and naturalness, and the dialogue made even the most outrageous events seem commonplace and normal. I learned many years later that Vic and Sade programs were written entirely by Paul Rhymer, considered one of radio's best writers, a man I wish I could have known.

Beside Rhymer and a few other writers, most of the day time soaps we listened to, when we had time, were written and produced by Frank and Anne Hummert..

E. Frank Hummert was a principal in the Blackett-Sample-Hummert Chicago Advertising Agency. Anne Ashenhurst, joined the agency as a copywriter where she impressed everyone with her talent and many new ideas. Anne became an agency partner at 22 years of age in 1927 and 7 years later married Hummert, although he was more than 25 years her senior. I read, but don't remember where I read the story, that Anne was earning $100,000 a year during the worst of the Depression.

After their first major success, Just Plain Bill, the Hummerts followed with Ma Perkins, Backstage Wife and Young Widder Brown. I liked Ma Perkins, the owner of a lumber yard. She reminded me of the mother of one of my boyhood friends. The handyman "Shuffle" was always getting into scrapes with problems Ma had to straighten out. Shuffle reminded me of a man who worked off and on for several years for my dad.

Mr. and Mrs. Hummert also produced many radio drama series, including Amanda of Honeymoon Hill, Front Page Farrell, John's Other Wife, Judy and Jane, Mr. Chameleon, Mr. Keen, Tracer of Lost Persons and Our Gal Sunday. Some of these soaps stayed on the air for many years. I remember listening to a few of them on my car radio many years later.

The Hummerts had as many as 18 separate 15-minute serials airing for a total of 90 episodes a week. Most programs originated in Chicago although the Hummerts had moved to New York.

Most of the Hummert plots underlined the gap between the wealthy and the aspiring middle class, bringing comfort to millions of listeners who were struggling with the reality of deprivation during the Depression. Ma Perkins and the other shows portrayed many of the same problems listeners were living with.

From their estate in Greenwich, Connecticut, Anne Hummert delivered a large weekly word count, outlining all of the plot twists for all of her programs. She farmed out the writing to script writers, known as "dialoguers", who embellished her synopses into complete scripts for the soap operas. The Hummerts shunned the spotlight, were very seldom seen in public and didn't give interviews. They each worked 14 hour days seven days a week and became immensely wealthy. When Anne died at 91 it was reported that she was billionaire.

When I read the story of the Hummerts in the magazine "Radio" I was even more anxious to get in that business some day. I wished at the time and wish now I could have met Frank and Anne Hummert. No wonder I grew up thinking Chicago was the center of the Universe. It certainly was the center of mine.

During the 1970s I employed a copywriter who had been one of the actors in the Chicago soaps. Malcome "Mac" Meacham had worked on several programs each day. He told us he would rush from one studio to another in the Merchandise Mart to portray different characters in different shows.

Probably the most remembered radio event of the depression occurred on Halloween 1938. It was the Orson Wells broadcast of The War of the Worlds that shook an entire nation with its realism. The first 30 minutes were delivered with no commercial interruptions but with vivid descriptions "directly from where it was happening" of an invasion of the

United States. So most listeners thought they were listening to a news broadcast of an invasion of alien Super Beings. I did not hear the original broadcast but listened to rebroadcasts a couple times. Many years later one of my copywriters, Patricia Cummings, used part of the Wells program in a bank commercial: "There were no 'green men' ...the only thing green at The Bank of Commerce is your money. Keep it safe with a Bank of Commerce insured Savings Account". I thought Pat was stretching the point a bit but the bank really liked the spot.

XVIII

I was 13 during the summer of 1934 when I spent a couple weeks with my grandparents in Chicago. It was during this stay in the city's Garfield Park neighborhood that I made my one and only visit to the Chicago World's Fair. I went there alone on the big red street car, making a single transfer. I was never afraid of doing something by myself. I always had complete confidence in my ability to act independently. My grandmother was reluctant to let me go but finally agreed, "If I would be careful", she said.

Street car transportation in Chicago in the 30s was the best in the country no doubt. If a person missed one car there was always another coming along just a few blocks down the street. Fare was seven cents with unlimited transfers. Street car transfers were also acceptable on the elevated trains.

Although I was completely unfamiliar with the big city street car routes I knew I could figure out how to get to the Fair once I was on my way. I had seen a map of routes to the Fair from different parts of Chicago and thought I could remember the one I needed. I had already seen many photographs and maps of the Fair itself in the newspapers and magazines. The Fair was widely advertised and publicized for a long time leading up to the Grand Opening.

So, I walked a couple blocks up Monticello Avenue from mom's grandparent's house and caught the street car going east on Chicago Avenue. About a mile or so, at State Street, I transferred to a car that took me south to 12th Street on the near south side of the Loop. From there it was an easy walk to the entrance to one of the most electrifying experiences of my early life. I was totally enthralled by the magnitude of the elegant art deco buildings and the excitement of the huge throng of enthusiastic visitors. I once read in the Chicago Tribune that people were coming from all over the world to visit this spectacular Fair, held during the worst of the Great Depression.

People walked or rode, seated sideways, in trains of five open cars pulled by General Motors light trucks. Above, the twin towers of the Sky Ride dominated the deep blue sky with the color broken only by a few scattered cumulus clouds. I knew it would be a thoroughly great day.

Inside each building was a wonderland just waiting to be explored by a 13 year old. I started at one end of the grounds and stopped at every building and exhibit on the west side of the fair, then worked my way back through the east side.

Above, I could see the Sky Ride gondolas shuttling back and forth full of passengers. I saw that each brightly colored gondola was named for characters from the Amos 'n Andy radio program. Beside the two main characters, Amos and Andy, I saw Kingfish, Madame Queen and Lightening, Others from the cast were Brother Crawford and Algonquin J. Calhoun, but I don't remember seeing their names on the gondolas.

I didn't even think about a ride up there because I didn't have enough extra money for a ticket and I didn't want to miss any of the exhibits on my limited time. And, I had flown quite often with my dad at our local Sky Harbor Airport.

While, because of age, I was not allowed in the famous Sally Rand Fan Dance Show, I did see one special attraction that made a big and lasting impression. It was a water carnival with gorgeous girls in colorful swim suits performing spectacular feats of water acrobatics. Like the later movies featuring Esther Williams, these young women would plunge in formation from bright colored bars near the ceiling down to the water, and then surface in ballet style, that totally engrossed and fascinated this young man from Northbrook.

When the show was over, the circular floor we stood on began to rotate toward the exit. It moved the audience out of the building, making way for new viewers. Not me. I pushed my way to the front along a small wall next to the water and, putting my arms on the railing, lifted my feet and let the floor move underneath me. So I saw the entire cavalcade of swim stars again.

By 9 o'clock or so I had seen all I could take in and was ready to catch the street car back home. It was dark now and I could see the blinking lights in the silhouetted buildings along Michigan Avenue in the distance. Would I remember my way back to Monticello Avenue?

As I approached the north exit my anxiety, which was really not much, was relieved when I saw my Uncle John waiting for me at the gate. My grandmother had sent him to find me, saying later that she couldn't believe I would stay so long after dark and was concerned about me. But who wouldn't want to spend the entire once-in-a-life-time-day at the magnificent Chicago World's Fair?

.

XIX

The years of the Great Depression were very busy ones for the movie industry. All the movies I remember seeing came from Hollywood. Most of the kids I grew up with knew the names of the most popular stars. We boys had our favorite cowboys and the girls skimmed the movie magazines for pictures and stories of their favorites.

I knew the names of many of the Hollywood Studios and was very interested in seeing the studio's trade mark opening at the beginning of each movie. I particularly liked the Universal spinning globe and stars. I liked the Columbia trade mark too because it meant my favorites, The Three Stooges might be coming on. I didn't know that one day, many years later, I would have as a friend, the niece of the Stooges' Moe, Shemp and Curley. I met Rhea Sallin while I was writing this book. At the time Rhea was also writing a biographical book. It was the story of Curley's life and career in motion pictures. Curley, the youngest in the family, died while still a young man. Rhea has favored me with a couple pages and I am very interested in reading the entire book.

I saw several movies in the 1930s at the Alamo Theater on Chicago Avenue, a couple blocks from my grandparent's house. That was my favorite over the Famous, a smaller movie house down the street from the Alamo. The Famous showed movies that were called "second run", meaning they had been played previously in the bigger theaters. It was a good place to catch a movie I might have missed earlier. They charged less too. Famous admission tickets were 25 cents for adults and 10 cents for kids.

When I was at my grandparent's house I quickly became friends with the kids in the neighborhood. Many times I went out with them and delivered printed flyers that advertised the newest coming attractions at the Alamo and Famous. We received passes, the number depending on how many flyers we distributed. The kids in those days were very honest and actually did put out the flyers, mostly on front porches. If one, maybe smaller kid, wasn't able to fill his "quota" others would help by putting flyers out for him so he got a pass too.

In Northbrook our family, as well as most of our neighbors, saw almost all our movies at the Theatro de Lago in "No Man's Land". No Man's Land was a strip of unincorporated terrain just north of Wilmette. The single business there was the magnificent movie house, "Theater of the Lake". Wilmette, Winnetka, Hubbard Woods and the other towns on the North Shore had banned movies. The result was No Man's Land and the Theatro de Lago. Most people simply called the theater "No Man's Land." Just like the movie palaces in Chicago, with their gigantic colorful lobbies, magnificent huge auditoriums and balconies, the Theatro de Lago was equal in every way.

Movie going when I was kid was an event. As we entered the lobby we saw the elaborate displays of coming movies with posters and pictures of the stars.

One display stands out in my memory more than others. It too was in the big lobby of No Man's Land. A popular movie Dinner at Eight was being promoted by setting up a big dinner table with eight places. Each setting appeared very glamorous in the bright lights coming from the ceiling, making the tall glasses and silverware glitter and sparkle. It was very impressive even to a kid.

I don't remember seeing the movie and when I looked it up and found who was in the cast I don't think my dad and mother would have gone to see the movie either. The film had many stars, John Barrymore, Wallace Beery and Jean Harlow among them. The actors and actresses in the movie, I learned later, were each under contract to Metro-Goldwyn-Mayer Studio.

MGM films were generally highly promoted and very popular. Dinner at Eight was a social comedy and I know my dad, who spent a lot of time smoking in the lobby when we watched any movie, would have been thoroughly bored with this one. The storyline about wealthy people with business problems because of the Great Depression would have been very boring to me and my brothers as well as our father..

I took an early dislike to any MGM movie. I did not like that studio's films because I felt MGM movies were too much about romance and not enough action.

This dislike even extended into my adult years. For example: After the Second World War I read the serialized story in Colliers Magazine about Jimmy Doolittle and the B-25 bomber raid on Japan in 1942, soon after the Japanese attack on Pearl Harbor. I was absorbed in the story of the long and arduous training these pilots went through, probably because of my own service in the Naval Air Corps. I could hardly wait for the next edition of the magazine each week. When the MGM movie, "Thirty Seconds over Tokyo", based on Colliers story, came out I was anxious to see how they had filmed that grueling training period.

I was shocked at the abomination MGM called a movie! The entire storyline concerned the pilots and their wives, how they lived and their various problems and love affairs. There was almost nothing about the tough training that took up most of the story in Colliers. It didn't occur to me that the studio had no doubt researched their potential audience and that probably the movie gave people what they really wanted, romance and a few minutes away from the cares of the world. People were really more interested in what the star, Van Johnson, was doing than Jimmy Doolittle. I never went to see a MGM movie again.

Going to the Movies was a special treat for our family as for most families. In the big lobby we got our first experience with Air Conditioning. The movie palaces were air conditioned at a time when artificial cooling was new and most homes did not have it.

It didn't matter, as far as the story was concerned where a person came into the theater. The movies were produced in a way that made it simple to catch on to the storyline no matter when you came in. After awhile I would hear, "this is where we came in", and some people would get up and leave the theater.

The really big movie house like the Chicago, State-Lake and Oriental were in the Loop. The Loop is an area in downtown Chicago bounded by the elevated tracks. The tracks are overhead on Lake Street, Clark Street, Jackson Boulevard and Wabash Avenue.

The Oriental lived up to its name. The doorman wore a turban and long silken costume and a pretty girl in an Arabian Nights dress presided over the foyer.

Chicago had some of the biggest and most luxurious movie palaces all over the city. Even neighborhood movie palaces were really just that, palaces. The Alamo where I went often was just one of many throughout the city. The most supreme movie house of all is the Chicago Theatre on State Street. The State Lake Theater is directly across the street.

The Chicago, with its gigantic marquee spelling out the word Chicago seats 3,800 and has an interior modeled on Louis 16th's Versailles Palace. It is magnificent.

Once I went to apply for a job there as an usher. The employment office was inside the stage door, half way down the alley along side the theater. There was a single line of young men from the stage door down the alley and two blocks down State Street. I was still in high school and most of those in line were older men so I gave up the plan.

Watching a movie in one of Chicago's movie palaces was a very pleasant experience. When you enter the semi-darkness, soft music puts one immediately at ease. The huge screen is not seen yet. It is covered by two curtains. One is a thin scrim behind the heavier colorful curtain. As the lights dim to near darkness the front curtain is slowly pulled aside. Music from the yet unseen silver screen begins and the movie studio trade mark logo shows on the white, almost transparent scrim. After a few bars of music the scrim is pulled bank too and the movie begins. It was all very dramatic and I enjoyed it every time.

If there was a stage show, especially featuring one of the big name bands like Benny Goodman, Glenn Miller or one of the other big bands, the opening was even more spectacular.

I would actually watch in awe as from behind both closed drapes the featured band would start playing their theme song as some young kids in the audience would begin loud clapping, whistling and stomping their feet. When we were feeling supreme anticipation, both curtains would be opened at once and the show began.

At the Chicago, and I never saw this in any other theater, as the curtains parted the band would come up from below to stage level. There was nothing like it and I never got tired of the anticipation and excitement of those shows.

Although most movies were in black and white Technicolor was introduced in the late 30s, and although very expensive, used in a few "block buster" films. The one I remember most was Gone with the Wind. It was in Technicolor and while still in production received a great deal of publicity in newspapers and magazines, especially in the many movie magazines. I remember at lot of speculation as to who would be the leading man. The book by Margaret Mitchell was widely read (I didn't read it) and Clark Gable seemed to most readers to be the overwhelming choice to play the leading man, Bret Butler.

I recall seeing the movie only after it had been shown for several months, maybe a year, I was amazed at the beauty of the color, especially a scene where the camera pulled back to reveal a big group of wounded people, soldiers and others. Although I knew many of the soldiers far in the background were dummies the scene was so real I remember it to this day.

146

Soon other studios began shooting in color, Warner Color was one of many, but none came even close to Technicolor.

Now, the great movie days, when pictures were made by what was called the studio system, are gone forever. The few remaining big Chicago movie theaters merely project film or digital video, no different than the mall theaters. But I can still see and hear the whole scene in memory that will remain with me forever.

Those movie experiences ended when the Great Depression was finally over. To me and my brother Elmer, our brother Paul died in 1992; it was a privilege to have lived through those wonderful years.

One Winter Sunday afternoon I was home alone. My mother and father and two younger brothers had probably gone to Chicago to visit my grandparents. I was running the radio dial up and down the numbers when I stumbled on a remote broadcast from the Piccadilly Circus Lounge in the Roosevelt Hotel in New York City. It was The Adrian Rollini Trio. They filled my room with the most magnificent music I ever heard. Rollini played the vibraphone, or vibes, accompanied by a guitar and string bass. I knew what I wanted to do with my life from then on. I listened to the 15 minute remote every possible Sunday afternoon. I could imagine myself no less than the star of the Piccadilly Circus Lounge.

Owning a set of vibes myself seemed impossible at the time. I was 15 years old, in my first year in high school, but I could dream. Dream I did, and listen to Rollini I did, and later when my summer job at the golf course allowed me to save part of the cost of the instrument my dad gave me the rest of the money and bought me a series of lessons at the Lyon & Healey Music Store in Chicago. I never attained the perfection of my idol but I became pretty good.

There was a popular local radio program broadcast in the Chicago area on Sunday afternoons. It was the Morris B. Sachs Amateur Hour, a program similar to the popular Major Bowes Amateur Hour on Network Radio. I had formed a trio of musicians with me playing the Vibes, Billy Christman on guitar and Roy Christiansen playing the string bass.

We auditioned and gained a spot on the show. The program originated live from a studio in the Merchandise Mart. The radio audience would vote by mail for their favorite. We came in second, beaten out by a tap dancer. Our prize was a man's Gruen wrist watch.

Our trio also appeared at local clubs and social functions and schools and since we couldn't divide the watch we sold raffle tickets at our performances and split the money 3 ways. We would decide the raffle date after we had sold enough tickets.

The big day turned out to be one of the PTA meetings at Grove School. My Uncle John conducted the drawing, putting all the tickets in a big cardboard box. He had a local school teacher pick out the winner while blindfolded. I thought it rather a coincidence that the winner of the watch turned out to be Uncle John's brother, my other Uncle Thorsten.

In 1935 I graduated from Grove School in a class of ten kids. It was the end of innocence. It was also the end of my interest in the Book of Knowledge volumes in Grove School. Up until graduation I had been an assiduous reader, devouring all the information on every subject I could find in the book's pages. That all ended when I left the 8th grade. I never really returned to such intense interest until I was successful in my own business and had reached the age of about 45.

The fall after graduation I started high school at Northbrook High and the first year was particularly unpleasant. From a "big wheel" at little Grove School I became a non-entity at what seemed to me a big high school full of all kinds of new activity. I was lost in the crowd of rowdy, uncouth, and what I thought were ignorant and ill-bred town kids. One guy I remember in particular was George Kratchovitch who kept hitting me on the back of the head with a book.

I was a skinny kid then, but one night many, many years later during my drinking days, I ran into George in a Waukegan Road tavern. It was about 3 am and I had been drinking heavily much of the night. When I saw George at the end of the bar I told one of our former school mates sitting at the bar about my high school experience with George and that I was going to get even. I might even have said I was going to kill him. I was drunk and could very well have made a threat I would really never mean seriously. But I never forgot the hits on the head and now I was not skinny any more, weighed about 200 pounds and knew I looked pretty rugged. George was scrawny and I never realized until then how small he was. Of course I had no intention of doing anything to him, but when I looked around, George was gone. He had ducked out the back door. I never saw him again. George had a younger sister named Martha who I thought was kind of cute.

I never attended any dances or other social events at Northbrook High. I didn't know how to dance and there was no one to teach me. I never felt I fit in at school until my 4th year. I felt like I was an outsider looking in at what the others were doing. I was happy while in class because I felt I was learning something valuable.

As a youngster I was often quite fearful of what I thought to be beings from a spirit world. I was nervous when in our house alone at night. I thought the upstairs storage rooms that were located on each side of the hallway leading to the bedrooms were dangerous for me at night. I never had these fears before about the age of 14 or 15. I still remember the night I came home from neighbor Teddy Marbet's house and found our house dark because my parents and brothers were still out. I was afraid to go in alone and went back to Marbets until I knew family had returned home. Writing these admissions makes me wonder if someone frightened me in early years with "ghost stories" that made me fearful. Perhaps growing up living so close to the cemetery located next to our property caused my fear. I suppose I will never know the reason. Now there is no time, day or night, that I have the slightest fear of anything or any person. I believe what FDR said in 1932, "The only thing we have to fear is fear itself".

XX

The mid nineteen thirties were often called "Dustbowl Days". A time of drought and wind that lasted close to 10 years. Lack of rainfall and fierce wind caused huge dust clouds that often blackened the entire sky. The effect of the devastation caused by the lack of rain, primarily in the southern Plains States, was felt all over the world, and the disastrous dust storms helped prolonged the Great Depression throughout the globe.

The severe drought hit worst in about 1931, coinciding with the deepening Depression. By 1932 there were 14 dust storms and that was just the beginning. The reason thousands suffered from the dust storms was because for millions of years the prairie grasslands of the Plains States lay undisturbed. Bison herds that were as much as 75 miles in length grazed on the prairie grasses. But when the land was settled by farmers and ranchers, their deep cutting plows turned the prairies into farmland and America became an agricultural exporter. The ready rainfall allowed the rich farmlands to produce abundant crops of wheat. The Great War of 1914 accelerated the expansion and prosperity of the Plains States.

Then in the early 1930s the rains stopped. Farmers continued to plant wheat but nothing grew. The grassland cover that once held the soil in place was gone. The weather pattern had changed too. Deep low pressure cells caused strong winds to whip across the plowed fields until the sky would become black with dust.

In the Chicago newspapers I saw many pictures of the storms with graphic descriptions of the suffering and growing poverty of the dust bowl. I don't remember reading about financial help from any government agency as would be the case today.

The dust storms would last for days. Houses would be thick with dust and farmers would string rope or wire between the house and barn in order to find their way between the buildings during a bad storm. A 14 year old boy was lost in a dust storm and found dead along the road the next day by his parents. The worst storm of all, on Sunday the 14th of April 1935, is written about today as Black Sunday.

I remember many days when the dust reached our Chicago area although we were many miles east of the worst storms. The dust in the sky would cause the sun to cast an eerie dull light on the landscape. My mother was constantly reminding us to keep the windows closed and close the doors quickly when we went in or out. It seemed that no matter how careful we were our house always needed dusting.

Northern states, like North Dakota and Wyoming, were not quite as badly hit, but the effect of the wind and heat, and the resulting agricultural devastation, was still a factor in prolonging the Depression in those states also.

People in Kansas, Nebraska, Oklahoma, New Mexico and Texas began to move out. Two hundred thousand eventually moved out of the wind and dust and went west. Many moved to California. Much of the time the newcomers were not welcome. California was suffering through the depression as well. Los Angeles Police Chief James E. Davis once sent 125 policemen to patrol the borders of Arizona and Oregon to keep "undesirables" out. As a result, the American Civil Liberties Union sued the city.

John Steinbeck wrote his well known and popular book The Grapes of Wrath in 1939, during these awful days just before the rains came back. Several other writers chronicling the era published their first works at that time. Much of the literary work of the 1930s that I read in school and at home "focused on the rejection of the notion of progress and a desire to return to an earlier age of purity and simplicity", a quote from US History Sparknotes.

John Steinbeck's Grapes of Wrath glorified a simple rural way of life. Jack Conroy's The Disinherited, a 1933 chronicle of an average industrial worker's life in the Depression Era, conveyed disillusionment and cynicism. William Faulkner also emerged as an important American writer, examining southern life in novels such as A Light in August, published in 1932, and Absalom! Absalom! published in 1936.

Although I read most, if not all, of these rather depressing books I was never influenced toward the communistic ideal the books suggested. I liked my life the way it was.

Even with bad news piling up all around I remember hearing news reporters with positive upbeat inflection in their voices. Adolph Hitler was also on the radio a lot then too. I don't know if any of the kids bothered to read Mein Kampf although there were copies in the school library. I didn't read it either until many years after the war.

When I came to California in the 1970s I met people who still remembered their trip out west and how lucky they felt to be away from the wind and dust and oppressive heat.

I became acquainted with several people whose families originally settled in the San Fernando Valley area of Los Angeles. During the Second World War a popular song about "Settling down and never more roam, and make The San Fernando Valley My Home" was played in juke boxes all over the country. The song is still heard occasionally. The lyrics to another dust bowl song went like this: "Dear Okie, if you see Arkie, tell 'em Tex is got a job for 'um out in Californy, raking up gold, all he needs is a shovel".

Still, most of the folks in the southern plains simply stayed where they were all during the worst of the blinding dust windstorms. Eventually the weather pattern changed again, rains returned, and the wind blew less violently. Those hardy dustbowl veterans who stuck it out confidently rebuilt their homes and farms once again and many of their descendents still live there today.

Through the years I have been privileged to know several "Okies". One lady, Eleanor Medsker from Shawnee, was going to be my wife when she suddenly and unexpectedly passed away. Her family was some of the hardy people who had stayed in Oklahoma in the face of bad odds.

My future wife, Jean Daniels, was growing up in Rock Springs Wyoming during the Depression and Dust Bowl Days and remembered only hearing about, not experiencing, the dust storms occurring in other states.

There was a Federal Government program called The Shelterbelt Project that called for large-scale planting of trees across the Great Plains, stretching in a 100-mile wide zone from Canada to northern Texas. Plan was to protect the land from erosion. I remember as a teenager, when I hitch hiked through the prairie states, seeing rows of those trees bending in the wind.

I heard that hoboes and "men of the road" traveling in search of work would camp along side the trees to be out of the fierce wind. The trees were the type that would offer protection alright because I saw their branches and leaves extend almost to the ground. In between the trees numerous bushes had been planted as well. I could see the land had been extensively re-plowed into furrows, although I didn't know the reason was to prevent the soil from blowing away. I thought that part of the country was pretty desolate and useless because I was used to the seemingly endless acres of corn that grew in Illinois and Iowa.

There was some better news in 1937 but the '37 upturn led to a deeper recession that lasted from the fall of '37 through most of 1938. Never the less, I remember my dad contracted with a Ford dealer in Highland Park to trade in his year-old Ford for a new one annually for one hundred dollars cash. The other Ford dealers located closer to our home complained bitterly to my dad and the Ford Motor Company.

It seems each dealer had a protected sales area and old Henry Ford was more interested in sales than enforcing the rules.

In the fall of 1939 the rains came to the southern plains again at last, finally bringing an end to the drought.

1939 was also the year I graduated from Northbrook High School. Economic prospects had become some what brighter by 1939. Dad's peony business at Glenbrook Gardens was good. Florists were buying more and more peony buds were being put in cold storage for sale in the fall.

In the roadside stand Dad had built so people could drive up and buy flowers, peonies sold for 50 cents a dozen. The summer of 2013 I saw peony buds in a California supermarket priced at three dollars for three buds. Peonies do not grow here in California's warm climate. But I have seen them thriving in other western states such as Wyoming where the altitude is over 5000 feet and the ground freezes in winter.

XXI

During the time I was between 13 and 17 I often caddied at either the University Country Club which was located in back of our property, or Sportsman's Golf Course, situated right across Dundee Road from us. Sportsman's was where Knoll's and other farms had been when we moved in and dad started the peony farm. It was a 27 Hole semi-public course while the University was private and was in existence well before we came there. The 14th fairway of University ran parallel to the back of our property, but quite a distance from our house.

When I applied for a job as a caddy at the University Club the caddy master gave me a metal badge with the number 4. I was aware that none of the other boys I went to school with caddied there. I soon found out why they didn't. The regular caddies were tough kids brought out from the poor, rough neighborhoods of Chicago. They were driven out by fathers who often caddied with their sons. I was very timid and the first time I was out on the course I had a feeling of extreme loneliness when I could see our house in the distance. But only that first time as a caddy, never after, although I was soon a regular caddy at the golf course.

The Chicago kids were all quite a bit older than me and very unfriendly. They thought I was taking jobs away from those who needed the work for the money. They were all poorly dressed while I wore a new pair of corduroy pants. I never told any of the city boys I lived next door to the golf course. I was surprised when one more friendly kid told me proudly that his father let him keep half of what he earned. Things must have been pretty bad in the part of Chicago where he lived.

My brothers Elmer and Paul caddied also sometimes. Paul was really too young but persuaded our dad to let him try. Paul was the most ambitious of the three of us.

The University 12th fairway was a "dogleg" to the left. Players had a choice, they could either hit the first drive about

100 yards straight ahead and take their second shot 90 degrees left toward the green. If they were confident they could make it, they could drive the ball over the field between the tee and green and save a shot.

But that was very risky because an old mean farmer who owned that property patrolled the corner, armed with a big shotgun. He was out there all day and picked up all the golf balls that landed on his land. He would not give the balls back even if they players offered to pay and if they approached too close to the small barbed wire fence he would threaten them with the shotgun. His property had never been farmed so was full of oak and hickories and rattle snakes.

In back of the cemetery adjoining the west side of our land was a rather low lying spot that dad used as a junk yard for old trash that would be hauled away later. I used to walk from the University caddy shack and club house past that junk on my way home. There was no fence between the lane the led to the shack and our property. One afternoon I saw a brief case on top of the junk that hadn't been there before. Of course I was going to investigate but three tough looking kids who I didn't know were walking behind me yelled, "Hey kid. Get out of here". One of them picked up the brief case, which I could tell by the way they were familiar with it, had been left there by them. It must have contained something they stole or maybe they stole the brief case itself from one of the club member's car. University Club members were wealthy men from the University Athletic Club in Chicago. They owned and operated the private golf course and all had huge expensive golf bags full of clubs. They drove high priced new cars too. The brief case looked expensive to me. I never saw those kids again and was glad they didn't come back to caddy.

Not long after the brief case incident the tough Chicago kids stopped coming out. Soon after that the club was closed and the course and club house never used again. The land lay abandoned for many years after the club closed. Even after I grew up and moved away it was still uncut tall grass and the beautiful greens and sand traps hardly recognizable. In winters the entire golf course would be covered with a layer of ice which made for wonderful skating, although in some places tufts of grass would stick up.

By the time the kids from Chicago stopped coming out I was caddying at Sportsman's. I was a lazy kid who didn't like caddying and once in awhile I would skip going to the golf course and alibi that there were no caddy jobs that day.

Once when I was walking down Dundee Road from Sportsman's the caddy master, Homer, came along and picked me up in his car and took me back to the golf course. The man I had caddied for told Homer I had stolen something from him, I guess it was from the golf bag. I was so frightened I never did remember. After being questioned they could tell I was innocent. Stealing anything was something I would never do but since I was so scared I didn't know what to say, but to deny it. When I was cleared and free to go I was so unnerved I took one big step from the club porch to the ground, missing several other steps. I could have been hurt but luckily wasn't.

Later I became the starter on the first tee at Sportsman's. I liked that job and made more money than as a caddy. My job was to take down names of foursomes and call out the name when previous golfers were far enough down the fairway to avoid being hit. On very busy weekends I was able to make a little more money by moving the names up the list for a couple bucks. But when the manager found out I had to quit doing that.

I had taken the place of a young man who had a car I really liked. My goal was to own one some day. It was a 1932 Ford Model B Roadster. His name was Jimmy Duchamp, about 25 or so, He was a heavy drinker for a young man and on weekends would have bad hangovers. The women cooks in the clubhouse would supply him with lots of coffee before he went to work. He was a very likeable young man. Unfortunately, on one of his nights out he got drunk and fell asleep on the side of the road and another car crashed into his and killed him. Many years later I had a 1929 Ford Roadster but always wanted a '32.

During the1930s many golf courses and restaurants had slot machines in back of the locker rooms and in back of dinning rooms. I would often watch the players and when I felt a slot was ready to pay off I would put in a coin and often won a little money. But I was never a gambler, never played any games of chance and even when in later years had a Nevada Casino as an ad agency client, never had any interest in gaming except advertising and promoting the client's business.

Before I got the job as starter I got the idea of building a two wheel cart that players could put golf bags in and pull along behind them. I had no money for wheels or other parts but the drawing I made looked quite similar to the actual carts that were manufactured some years later.

I did not discuss my idea with my dad or anyone else. I didn't have that kind of a relationship with my father. In fact it was not until I was in my late 40s that my dad came to one of my ad agency Christmas parties in Salt Lake City that he knew how successful I had been lucky to become. I know he was impressed and told my brother Paul how proud he was of me. Neither of my brothers had a close relation to our father that I know of, but neither did any of the other kids and their fathers. That was the way it was in those days.

Another time I had the idea for a machine that would hold Coke bottles which could be automatically ejected with the insertion of a nickel. I described that idea to a few friends whose reaction was, "Are you stupid, your machine would have to be six feet tall'. Well, as it turned out they are six feet tall, maybe more.

My dad had a great workshop on the second floor of the garage. Often I would decline to go with the family on Sunday to visit some friends because I wanted to use the time to build my "inventions". But I had no way to keep my diving helmet from leaking, no glue, so it leaked when I tried it in the pond. I did actually build a collapsible fishing boat that could be put in back of a car but couldn't seal it so while it would really fit in a car, my invention leaked and sunk.

For some time I had been trying to do some serious romancing with one of the girls in school who was a couple years older than me. We had done a little hugging and some kissing in the backyard of her house. Another kid in school had the same idea with another girl whose parents were friends of my family. The girls both said they wouldn't hear of it. But after many attempts and lots of kissing, both girls finally agreed.

Behind the school yard was the small pond dad had dug. He also planted willow trees around one side of the pond and there was a wooden bench in the small forest of willows. It was pleasant back there and I felt it an ideal spot to have my first experience of something but I really didn't know what was going to happen. I was about 14 and my girl was 15. I didn't know how experienced she was. I had none of a serious nature.

We arranged for the four of us to spend some time together the night of the next PTA meeting, when our parents were all engaged in school stuff. The girls said they would bring a couple blankets. When the night of the PTA meeting arrived the girls brought the blankets in their parent's cars and we headed for the pond. But then disaster struck.

Disaster struck in the form of a stink bomb. There was a kid in school named Edwin "Curley" Curth, who was always experimenting with chemicals and building gadgets no one but Curley himself could understand. This time he had made a gigantic stink bomb and was going to set it off in the basement of the school house during the PTA meeting.

Just as the four of us got to the middle of the school yard the bomb went off and black smoke and an awfully foul smell came up and out from the basement. Parents and teachers rushed out on to the porch. A friend of my dad's, Mr. Christiansen, announced with a broad Danish accent, "It's a stink-bum". Parents started calling for their kids. We boys and the girls had to rush back to the school as fast as we could. Our great plan came crashing down. The big night didn't happen. I never forgave that rotten Curley for ruining my night out. My girl got married a couple years later. I don't know who she married or who the other girl eventually married either.

My co-conspirator was Teddy Marbet who didn't go on to high school and shortly before the start of the Second World War went into the Army.

XXII

During the 1920s and 30s prohibition helped create the "Bank Gangsters", a type of outlaw similar to the stage coach robbers of the Old West. But these law breakers robbed banks, many in small towns, throughout America. Depression era outlaws, like Bonnie and Clyde, "Baby Face" Nelson, Ma Barker, and "Pretty Boy" Floyd, became legends, as their deeds included some of the wildest and deadliest stories ever to hit our Chicago Tribune and other newspaper front pages.

The Bank Gangsters became even more notorious during the Depression.

Among the infamous criminals of the 1930s John Dillinger was by far the most notorious. He was famous for his likable personality and charm. He would often flirt with the female bank tellers he was robbing and would sometimes leap over the counter, a stunt he imitated from the movies. Dillinger was finally named Public Enemy Number One.

I remember clearly the night of his demise shortly after he attended the Biograph Theatre in Chicago. After exiting the theatre the FBI were waiting for him and he was shot down as he tried to escape down a nearby alleyway. That hot muggy night stood out in my mind for many years. We had just returned from our summer home at Lauderdale Lakes. When we stopped at a local restaurant, dad picked up the late edition of the Chicago Tribune and read the gruesome story. My mother was disgusted with bystanders who dipped newspapers in Dillinger's blood for souvenirs.

There were many other outlaws of the 1930s who also came to a violent finish. Bonnie Parker and Clyde Barrow were ambushed in May, 1934. Barrow was killed instantly by a shot to his head and Parker, in the passenger seat, was sprayed with bullets immediately afterward. They were shot over 50 times even after they were dead, including numerous headshots on each corpse. The gruesome, story with many pictures, was printed in all our daily papers.

Ma Barker was infamous as the leader of the Barker-Karpus Gang. She was actually an elderly woman not involved in crime herself. Yet she was brutally murdered by being shot many times by FBI agents. Several years later I read an interview with Alvin Karpus who said Ma did know about the crimes committed by the gang but was not involved in any way. He said she was "too dumb".

Karpus kidnapped William Hamm Jr., the president of the Theodore Hamm's Brewery. Hamm's father was friends with President Franklin D. Roosevelt and as a result the FBI stepped in. Karpus was caught and sentenced to life imprisonment. He served his time in Alcatraz.

In our area, Roger "The Terrible" Touhy was well known even by the kids. In 1933, Al Capone had corrupt law enforcement officers arrest Touhy for the kidnapping of Hamm, even though evidence showed the Barker-Karpis gang did the crime. Nevertheless, Touhy and three others were indicted on kidnapping charges. They were found not guilty.

I knew about the whole story because for years Roger Touhy was big news in the northern Chicago suburbs. He was one of several Touhy brothers to live a life of criminal activity.

All this criminal news, with bank robberies reported almost daily, was every day fare during my days attending the one room Grove School. Kids knew the names of the most wanted because gangsters names hit the newspapers almost every day. I followed the news and even knew the location of the house Touhy lived in.

One day, right after Baby Face Nelson was shot to death, one of the kids walking through the high grass near Sky

Harbor Airport, found a 32 caliber revolver. While there was no connection to Baby Face's death, we all felt the gun had some criminal association.

XXIII

In the fall of 1937 I was about to start my 3rd year in high school. Someplace, I had discovered that we who lived outside the boundaries of any school district could attend any school in the state of Illinois. We were not restricted to any particular district. So I decided I would go to Highland Park High School instead of Northbrook.

When I told some of the other Northbrook students what I was going to do a few of them decided to go to Highland Park High too. Donald Graber, Freddie Weiseman and a couple of the Reeb kids were among them. I made a deal with Mimi Reeb, one of their older Reeb girls, to ride to Highland Park with her for a small fee. That arrangement didn't work out too well.

Just before school started I had my tonsils out for the second time. The first time was in that "hospital" in Wheeling owned by a quack doctor named Larsen. The job was botched and I had tonsillitis many times during the years and a constant cold during most winters. Part of the reason for the colds was because my Dad insisted on keeping the house very cold, probably to save on coal bills. Had my tonsils been removed correctly I would probably have eliminated many of my colds.

Shortly before the school year started Walt Thummel, a local tavern owner, told my Dad about a clinic in Chicago where what was left of my tonsils could be removed cheaply. Dad took me to the clinic and I had tonsils out again, but went home the same day very sick in the back seat of the car. This job was botched as badly as the first and one tonsil still remains in my throat.

Although my throat was extremely painful I started school in Highland Park anyway. Since I had no car I rode to school with Mimi and her brothers. Reebs had a 4-door Graham Paige car. After riding for a few weeks, I stopped giving Mimi the money my father had given me to pay them and Mimi refused to pick me up any more.

On the first Monday morning, after the Christmas and New Years Holidays, they whizzed right past me as I was standing along the road in front of our house. Those in the car looked straight ahead as if I wasn't even there, didn't give me a side glance. Mimi, who drove, stared straight ahead too with her mouth set firmly in a grimace, determined not to pick me up.

I never rode with them again and many afternoons after school I walked the entire five miles home. Sometimes I would walk to Ken Caldwell's house to get him to drive me the rest of the way home. He lived about half way between school and my folk's house.

But most mornings after the Reebs dropped me I usually hitchhiked to school along with Donald Graber, one of the other Northbrook students who had decided to attend

Highland Park High that year. I would walk, even in winter, about 2 miles to the Graber house. Donald, whose nickname was "Darky", and I would walk another half mile to Skokie Boulevard where he would stand on the east side of Skokie and I would stand on the other side, trying to get rides in opposite directions. One way went toward Highland Park and school, the other toward Chicago. So, we would either go to school that day or downtown to the movies, depending on the direction of our ride.

After almost being kicked out of school I had my first very bad migraine headache. It was a new experience for me and I became very sick with disturbed vision and a violent headache.

Although I had played the saxophone and clarinet in the Northbrook school band, I did not play in the band at Highland Park because I had no saxophone and the school didn't furnish instruments as they did at Northbrook. So I sat in a corner while the band rehearsed. No one, not even the conductor, questioned why I was sitting there doing nothing for an hour every few days. At first I felt embarrassed and like an outcast but soon got used to being an outsider.

May 6th, 1937 is a day I remembered for a long time, especially because of my interest in flying. While in class we heard the news over the speakers of the airship Hindenburg's fiery crash in Lakehurst, New Jersey. The same night the Chicago Daily News in a special edition carried pictures of the shocking disaster. The new newspaper wire services had made it possible for us to read in detail and see the photos of the sudden crash as the Hindenburg was attempting to land.

At first it was just a small flame that appeared on the outer cover at the rear of the dirigible. Within 34 seconds, the entire airship was consumed by fire. This trip was the first of the 1937 season for passenger service between Europe and the United States. It turned out to also be the last. Public interest in lighter than air travel ceased with this tragedy.

I read in one of the papers that the German builder of the Zeppelins asked the United States Government for permission to buy helium, since it is plentiful here as a bi-product of oil drilling. No helium was available in Germany. The story we heard was that President Roosevelt personally intervened and stopped the export of helium. Some commentators blamed Roosevelt for the Hindenburg crash. Because of his action the dirigible was filled with the highly flammable hydrogen. For the next several days the kids talked about the crash.

The Hindenburg was even more important than the latest Big Band record, but only for a little while. I had wanted to fly in a dirigible ever since I saw the big ship at Grove School a few years before.

During my junior year at Highland Park High School I listened every Monday night to the Lux Radio Theater, hosted by the famous movie producer Cecil B. De Mille. DeMille would open the program himself by announcing is a deep melodramatic voice, "Lux Presents Hollywood".

The program, sponsored by Lux toilet soap, consisted of shortened versions of popular motion pictures, generally with the same stars as the movie. Besides entertainment, the idea was to draw audiences to the movie houses. The commercials featured prominent female stars who proclaimed Lux to be their own special beauty soap. .

Every evening during summers of the late 1930s, about five o'clock, two huge dump trucks, one a few feet behind the other, would come roaring down Dundee Road past our house, going east toward Bach Town. It was the "Ebelsiser Twins", actually father and son who, despite their ages, looked identical with their bald heads. They had a trucking business hauling black dirt.

The son Don was married to Aline Johnson a young girl I admired many years before. She was half Jewish. Her mother was called Jew Johnson by everyone. Aline's father was Harry Johnson. Both parents, and daughter, were members of the North Northfield Church. Many years later, in 1945, after I returned from the Navy, I saw Aline in the church again. She was dressed rather shabbily.

During 1937-38-39 summers and spring vacations I worked for my dad on landscape jobs. I hated the work. I feel now that I had a generally dreary unhappy life as a youngster. I was not comfortable with my home life. I began to dislike the house we lived in, but don't know the reason for my discomfort. It was probably boredom. I wanted to get out in the real world, away from what I thought was a restricted life. I was frustrated because lack of money kept me from achieving any of my plans or ideas. As it turned out, when I did leave home I still had no money and it was a considerable length of time before I could put my first idea into action.

For the 1938-39 school-year I went back to Northbrook High. By now the kid who had harassed me had either graduated or moved away. Just before school started I met a girl named Marge who was very pretty and I thought would be going to school with me. When school started Marge was not there. I think she was one of the many girls who just didn't go to high school.

Although I didn't play in the Highland Park band, but sat in a corner while the band rehearsed, I played baritone saxophone in the Northbrook High School Band. In Highland Park I had no sax or clarinet and couldn't afford one, but Northbrook School owned and furnished the instruments. The year before Jack Magnuson had played the same instrument. I also played the clarinet in the Little German Band our Home Room teacher Miss Helen Dirks organized.

Soon after starting my last year in high school my Grandmother, Henny Doll, bought me a 1929 Essex car. At one time the car had been black, but ten years and the sun had turned it into a terrible dark gray color. The Essex was a smaller 4 cylinder version of the popular Hudson car. My grandmother paid $25 for the four door sedan.

The car ran OK, but blue oil smoke filled the inside of the car after driving a few miles. That was OK in warm weather because then I kept the windows open. After awhile the starter broke so I parked the Essex on a hill across the street from the school and coasted down until I got up enough speed to let out the clutch and start the engine. Other times I had to crank the engine. I drove it to school when I had money for gas and rode the school bus other times.

One of my classmates in Northbrook was Warren Harer, who always seemed to be a step ahead of us other boys. When I had the Essex, he had a fairly new Ford V-8. While we others caddied at the local golf courses he worked at an easier job in a gas station. Some of the boys went to work at the Asplundh tree trimming company. Warren dated and married the owner's daughter. I also went to Asplundhs one day but failed the tree trimming test. I was far too timid to climb the trees to cut off branches.

Warren went into the Army and when he came home again he had begun to refer to women as skin. He would say, "Let's go out and see if we can meet some skin", and so Skin became his knick name. Warren died in 2010. I would have bet he would outlive all the other kids in our 1939 graduating class. Maybe playing pinochle and drinking beer every day at Bartalmes' Tavern didn't secure the long life I was certain Skin would enjoy.

Another of my classmates was Freddie Weiseman whose father owned Weiseman's Tavern, a couple doors south of Louie Junkin's Shoe shop. Freddie also went to Highland Park High his 3rd year but didn't go back to Northbrook like I did. He graduated from Highland Park High School, went to law school and became one of Northbrook's best known lawyers. He gained a reputation for being able to get his clients out of drunken driving charges. He also started Northbrook's first newspaper.

During my last year in high school I frequently skipped school and went to downtown Chicago where I would go to the Gem Burlesque Theater on South State Street. During intermissions between the movie and the stage show, a man would pass up and down the aisles hawking various cheap products. One time I bought a safety razor but received only part of the razor.

After the Gem I would stop in a liquor store and buy a few pint bottles of wine which I would sell to the boys at school. I got in a jam once when a couple boys threatened me because I didn't deliver the wine they paid me for. The money they gave me for wine went for a ticket at the Gem. I later provided the wine they paid for.

At the time I was 18 or so years of age I would often stop in a bar or tavern for a cold beer, or have one with my dad. No one asked my age or for identification. I had no ID anyway. Illinois did not require a driver's license to drive a car and I didn't have a Social Security number yet. As far as drinking was concerned, if you were big enough you were old enough. I didn't drink very much anyway. It was only later when I began to work with a bunch of older "factory stiffs" that I drank more than I should have.

One day, when I should have been in school, I took a street car to Maxwell Street on the south side of Chicago's loop and bought a fairly good guitar for $6. Maxwell Street was full of small shops run by Jews. No matter what the cost of the item a buyer wanted, it was customary to bargain for a better price. Often, depending on the price of the item, this haggling went on a long time.

I learned to play the guitar fairly well, and with the attachment I made myself that held a large harmonica, began to entertain my friends. Kenneth (Joe) Caldwell, who attended the little North Northfield Church occasionally with me, played the mandolin and we formed a duet, playing in several amateur theatricals around town.

In June I barely had sufficient credits to graduate from high school. I had enough only because I received half a credit for playing in the band and a half credit for a class called business arithmetic. I had been unable to comprehend and pass algebra, geometry or physics in high school. But just three years later, while in the Navy Air Corps studying at Monmouth College, I passed each course with ease.

The president of the School Board, Max Hoffman, gave the primary commencement speech. His son was also a student at Northbrook High. Hoffman was later charged with some criminal activity. I don't know if he was convicted.

In early 2013 my sister-in-law Betty, who married my brother Elmer, had for years kept track of happenings in Northbrook informed me that I was the probably the sole survivor of the 1939 Northbrook graduating class. One other member of the class, Donald Hintz, was in a care provider home. I was no doubt the only one actively working. There had been 23 in the graduating class of 1939.

On September1st 1939, after Europe had been nervous for years about Hitler's plans, the German Dictator invaded Poland. It was the start of another World War in Europe. I didn't know, none of us did, that eventually the United States would be involved too.

XXIV

There was never any thought by me or my parents of me or my brothers attending college after high school. So I got a job at the Central Metallic Casket factory in Chicago where I worked as strike breaker. The company owner's nephew also worked at the factory, as well as Del Dobbins, a man who worked for my dad in the nursery business. Because of the threat of violence by the union and strikers we rode to work together in a big Buick. Often the union organizers would follow us to and from work, but never interfered with us.

One day I threw an apple from the 2nd story factory window at the pickets walking in front of the building. By pure luck I hit a big black union organizer right on the side of the head. This caused a big commotion for awhile, but no one knew I had thrown the apple so there was no trouble for me.

My job was to cut wooden pieces that were used to hang fabric in the caskets. Each piece was a certain length and the company had patterns which were duplicates of what I was making. One day I got the idea of making just one pattern 2 feet long with notches cut in the sides. I could then obtain the correct length for each piece by using the short pattern and notches in a certain order to measure and cut the correct ends and sides of the pieces. For example: two lengths of my pattern plus the second notch gave me the correct measurement for the casket sides. It saved time as I didn't have to pick up and lay aside each pattern as needed. I was severely reprimanded by the foreman boss who informed me in no uncertain terms that he was the pattern maker.

The man who owned the factory was named Forke, pronounced for-kee. He seemed to be fairly well to do and lived in Wheeling in a big house about 2 miles west of our home, Mr.Forke had a niece named Dorothy. I thought she was rather pretty, although older than me. Forke attended the local North Northfield Church. He gave a talk one time during which he spoke at length about the Kiwanis Club. I had never heard of this organization before and thought it must be quite an important association. When Forke died the company made a special casket for him that was constructed of copper with real silver seams.

After working a couple months on the job, the strike was settled and I was out of work as pattern cutter. The company offered me a job in the basement where the huge machines that cut the metal for the caskets were located.

The first thing I immediately noticed down there was that several of the workers were missing fingers, some a couple on each hand. This was dangerous work and not for me I could see that. I was to observe the operator doing the work the first morning and start operating the machine by myself that afternoon,

The task consisted of holding a big piece of flat steel at the edge of a huge punch press that would slam down and bend the metal into its proper shape. The idea was that the movement of the sheet, as the press came down, would push my hand out of harm's way. It worked OK for the operator but I shuddered every time the press came slamming down. At noon when we knocked off for lunch I left the factory and never went back.

During the strike there had been a small man who always yelled at me when I was coming or leaving the plant. He was nasty but I didn't pay much attention to him. One day after the strike was over and I had left the job, I came back to the factory for my last paycheck. I had my old Essex car and as usual it had no starter, so I cranked it each time. As I was standing in front of the car with the crank in my hand the little fellow who had harassed me came around the corner. I was a pretty big kid and he turned as white as the proverbial sheet. I just ignored him and he turned and went back into the building. Winter came and I had no job. There was nothing to do at home.

XXV

So, on the 20th of January, 1940 my dad decided I should enroll in the Civilian Conservation Corps. Why he did this I will never know. Perhaps I was a burden on the family finances, and I certainly wasn't doing anything useful around the house. I had been helping my dad in our basement by painting names of peonies on three by four inch wooden signs that were attached to metal poles which he placed in the show garden during the summer to identify the several varieties of peonies.

Entering the CCC began one of the most disagreeable experiences I ever had, certainly during my youth. I had no choice about enlisting. My dad simply decided one day I was to go in and there was to be no discussion or argument about it. He merely announced I was to enroll and took me down to Chicago on a cold winter day for enlistment. My dad did all the necessary paper work to get me enrolled. In fact we were called enrollees. The whole episode felt bizarre to me. I was 18 years of age, didn't have a job, and was not trying to find one. In my own defense I will say I was quite naive and I guess not ready for the adult world.

Also living out in the country a couple miles from town made kid jobs very scarce. Perhaps my dad felt the CCC would "make a man" of me? I don't know.

The CCC district where I was stationed was located in Glenview. The camp itself was situated about 4 miles south of Northbrook. I knew of the camp before hand because some years earlier a race riot had erupted between the Blacks and Whites in the camp. I don't remember if I ever did know what started the trouble. But now that I know more about race relations I suspect it had something to do with Negro men involved with White women.

Of course I hated every minute of that awful experience. I thought the young men enrolled in the CCC were some of the most loathsome people I ever encountered anywhere. I spent only a few nights in the barracks and they were truly dreadful. The coal stoves at each end of the barracks emitted the foul smell of cheap burning coal. The obnoxious odor permeated the entire barracks.

There was no ventilation because the whole barracks was closed tight against the winter. Several of the enrollees played their radios all night. For me, who was used to his own room and the quiet of the open country, this was a change of enormous proportions. The enrollees were a generally nasty and stupid bunch of individuals. One night the police came into the barracks and arrested a couple of them. I believe it was for car stealing.

Most of the enrollees has been involved with breaking the law and had been convicted of something. During the depression the county jail in Chicago was overloaded with prisoners. So, more times than not, for smaller convictions the guilty had a choice. Either serve a sentence of six months in the county jail or six months in the CCC. Six months was the normal period of enlistment.

The jobs we were supposed to do were landscaping the Skokie Lagoons, which had previously been known as the Skokie Slough, a marshland thousands of years old. I actually went out on the job one day. That was enough. I vaguely remember the project on that dreary cold wet day. It was a muddy hole and the CCC boys didn't seem to be working very hard. I left the camp after staying there a very few miserable days and nights, even though I had no place to go.

During the last week of January and all of February and March I wandered each day up and down through the suburban villages of Wilmette, Winnetka, Glencoe and Kenilworth along the Lake Michigan shore.

In those days the now long gone North Shore Electric Railroad ran two parallel routes north and south between Chicago and Milwaukee. One, the Shore Line Route, had tracks along Lake Michigan through the suburbs mentioned above. The other route ran to the west through Glenview, Northbrook and on to Milwaukee.

In 1975, while in Sacramento, California, I found and bought a book chronicling the history of the North Shore RR. On one page is a picture of a snow covered Wilmette Street on a cold January day in 1940. A North Shore snow scraper car is shown coming down the street. The weather is cold, cloudy and dreary. On the January day that picture was taken I could very well have walked down that same street. And at the very same moment, since it was one of the streets on which I wandered many times those unforgettable winter days. I have an eerie feeling even now when looking at this photograph.

I would walk many miles each day or hitch hike back and forth through the shoreline suburban towns. Some days I spent time visiting auto dealerships pretending I was a prospective car buyer.

One early morning while hitch-hiking on Sheridan Road I was picked up by some young people in a Ford Convertible. They had apparently been at an all night party. They were still half drunk and their car had a bashed in fender. They gave me a ride but I was glad to get away from them. It gave me a brief look at another side of life from the one I was living.

Many nights were spent in all-night movie houses in Chicago, sleeping, or trying to sleep, in the uncomfortable seats. It was a very difficult life those nights in the cold winter. But it was warm inside the theaters.

In my advertising agency by the 1960s I was able to afford the luxury of a large impressive personal office. (Advertising is Show Business too!) More than once, as I sat there at work I thought to myself, "Am I the same person who slept in all night movie houses once upon a time?"

The little CCC money I had came from the small cash I received each month. I don't remember what I got. The pay was $30 a month but some of it went to enrollee's family so I didn't get very much. This was a time when privates in the Army, the GIs, got only $21.

One nasty day when I was desperately hungry, I felt what I thought was a nickel in the lining of my overcoat pocket. A nickel would buy me a fair sized candy bar in those long gone days. But unfortunately I found it was only a button. I was truly sunk.

I remember quite clearly standing one time on Dundee Road in the dark cold near the front of our home. Through the window I could see my dad sitting comfortably in a big easy chair reading the evening paper.

Although I slept most of the nights in the all night movie theaters in Chicago, I spent one bitter cold night sleeping in the very small Kenilworth North Shore station. The station agent came in about 4 in the morning to stoke up the coal fire but he didn't kick me out. In those depression days there may have been others sleeping there at various times too.

In April I was finally able to leave the CCC when Sven Larsen, the Grove School janitor who also owned a green house, gave me a job working in his green house. I never could blame my father for my bad experiences because I realized he didn't know what had happened to the CCC since the days he knew of it as a good place for young unemployed men. In those earlier days the CCC boys built parks and camping facilities in various parts of the country. I saw some of them later during my travels throughout the West. I only blamed myself. I had strayed far away from my goal of owning my own business. I was in no position to advance my goal right then and had temporarily lost the vision.

XXVI

Soon after I came home after the CCC experience I constructed a display which I hoped to sell to a movie theatre in Highland Park, the town where I went to high school during the 1937-38 school year. The display consisted of large cardboard cutouts of the characters from the animated Disney cartoon film Pinocchio. I was too timid to try to sell the theater owner and totally unaware of the impracticability of trying to sell my display to a local theater owner in the first place. I also wrote the Walt Disney Studios who sent a nice reply saying they had their own promotion department. During these years

I also sent magazine covers I had designed to the publishers of the Saturday Evening Post and Colliers magazines. The artwork was very bad and of course was rejected. But I was trying once again.

I soon left Sven Larsen's green house job and took another with the Miller sod farm. They grew grass that was cut a few inches below the roots and rolled into sod that was later unrolled to make an instant lawn. My first job was loading heavy bags of Milorganite, a commercial fertilizer used on the large acres of grass growing on the farm. I also drove a big Fordson tractor, one with the very large metal back wheels, pulling several mowing machines.

I didn't make much money. My largest pay for a six day week was $25, one time. Mr. Miller paid me with checks he had received from his customers. I was lucky they were always good and none "bounced". Had they not been good I'm sure he would have paid me in cash, because he was an acquaintance of my Dad's and I went to school with his son and two daughters. One daughter was named Marylyn who I thought was pretty cute. Many years later at our a Northbrook high school reunion I saw her again. She was then a nice little old lady.

Mr. Miller was a German Catholic who had large war pictures cut from the Chicago Tribune hanging in his barn. He was proud of the advances the German Army was making through France at the beginning of the Second World War that had started in September 1939. I quit that job as soon as I could.

But before I left the job I would often stop on Saturday evenings after payday at a night club named Scarletts. I'm almost certain Scarletts was owned by the Chicago Mafia. One time I brought a dozen peony flowers from my dad's peony garden as a gift. Why I did this I don't know except I suppose I wanted to impress a young woman who worked there. When I presented the flowers to the bartender, who I had gotten to know a little, he made a big fuss by asking the other workers, "Who ordered these flowers?" He certainly did not intend to pay for them. I was too embarrassed to tell him I had brought them as a gift. I don't remember if I left them or took them home again but I never went to Scarletts after that experience.

Later that summer my dad got me a landscaping job in Glenview. The job consisted of general yard work like cutting grass and trimming hedges and flower beds. The man who was my boss was named Pete. One very hot day when I was working in the back yard the pretty young woman who lived there asked me if I would like a cold bottle of beer. Of course I did and when she brought it she invited me to sit on the porch with her and drink the beer. As I sat there enjoying my beer Pete came looking for me and when he found me on the back porch drinking beer with the lady of the house he fired me on the spot.

XXVII

One day in late August I had an especially bad migraine headache. In my early days of migraines I became very sick and my head throbbed with pain. I had to lie down and my mother would put hot towels on my face and eyes. I usually fell asleep and when I awoke I felt better and quite calm. I'm sure my migraines were caused from tension and they still are, even though I only have the strange shapes in front of my eyes with no headache.

Later that day I met Eleanora Kriski who was going to teach at Grove School. She lived in Chicago but looking for a place to stay during the school week.. My mother arranged for Eleanora to board at our home. She stayed with us during the week and went to her parent's home in Chicago on weekends. Eleanora was six years older than I was and taught the first through fourth grades.

From about the 2nd week she was there I began to experience a lonely feeling when she was away. This was the first time in my life I had ever missed any anyone. One day I noticed she was receiving letters in our mailbox from a man she had dated in Rockford where she had previously taught school. I am quite sure their relationship had ended about the time she came to Northbrook.

Eleanora and I hit it off very well right from the start. She was someone I had been looking for all my life. One evening soon after meeting her I had an appointment to meet a commercial artist who lived in Northbrook. I don't remember how I got the appointment, but the meeting was for a chance at a job in a Chicago commercial art studio. Eleanora went with me as far as the front door of the man's house. As I was about to ring the door bell she unexpectedly gave me a kiss on the cheek for good luck. Nothing came of the interview but I never forgot the kiss.

That winter we began to spend weekends together. On Saturday's I would go to her house in Chicago and we would take the Addison Street bus downtown in bitter cold weather to a movie. Being with Eleanora on the bus, or anywhere, was the very first time in my life I was truly happy.

The cold harsh winter of 1940 ended and an even colder 1941 began. Early in January I went on a couple sleigh rides with Eleanora and experienced extremely cold feet. Quite possibly I had no really warm boots.

The sleds were really long planks fastened to a couple 4 by 6 boards for runners. The whole contraption was pulled by an old car driven by a man named Harry Winter who I could see was more than a little interested in my girlfriend. But he didn't even talk to her. He just looked. During WW-2 years Winter escaped military service by working as an aid to Leighton Wilke, head of the Do-all Company. Do-all was heavily engaged in war production and became one of my future short term employers. Several Do-all employees as well as my brother Elmer were annoyed at Winter receiving this employment benefit.

By early spring Eleanora and I were spending even more time together. One evening Joe Caldwell arranged for a group of us to go horseback riding. In order to impress Eleanora I told her that I had quite a bit of riding experience. Actually, I had never been on a horse in my life. When we picked up the nags at the stable, Joe told the owner, in front of Eleanora, to give me a gentle horse because I had never ridden before. She didn't comment on my lie.

We rode to a local tavern on Milwaukee Avenue called the Green Duck. We drank a few beers and then rode back to the stables. I have never been on a horse since that night. It was probably obvious to my family I had a crush on Eleanora.

Eleanora continued to spend weekends with her parents in Chicago. She would come to our house on Sunday evenings. One time her brother and some of his friends brought her to the house. The bunch of us began playing the piano and singing somewhat loudly in the living room. I suppose the noise became annoying to my dad, or for some other reason he was upset, because just a couple minutes after they had all left dad announced that I had to make a choice. I would either go back in the CCC again or join the army. I was stunned.

At my dad's further insistence I went to the Chicago National Guard Armory one day and enlisted in The United States Army. I knew I had no other choice because I had no job and was just hanging around the house. But the army rejected me. I was judged to be underweight. I was a little over six feet tall and weighed 160 pounds. Eleanora and I were both very glad and happy that I didn't have to join the army, and we began to spend even more time together.

More than 70 years have elapsed since that episode and I am still as puzzled about my dad's reason for the army, as I am about my previously forced enlistment in the CCC. He didn't like Eleanora, in fact my dad disliked most intellectuals. I suspect the army was because he wanted me to get away from her.

When Eleanora bought a car I taught her to drive in a yard area where landscapers had removed the black soil. (They sold the soil to owners of the new homes in the area.) After learning how to drive, Eleanora moved back with her parents on the north side of Chicago and drove to her job at the school each day.

After that, as often as I could I would some how get from our home to town and catch the Milwaukee train to the Mairfair Station near Eleanora's house. After walks in the neighborhood we would hug and kiss in the apartment entrance before she went in. Then I would walk through a small park and catch the last train from Mairfair back to Northbrook. By then it was after midnight and I had a two and a half mile walk back home.

If I was lucky I would get a ride. That was when Northbrook's only policeman, Don Clavey, would meet the last train of the day out of Chicago. Don Clavey was high schoolmate David Clavey's father. As a courtesy, Mr. Clavey would take the one or two late train passengers home and then I had a ride too.

One day my dad told Mr. Clavey not to take me home any more and that was the end of my rides. Dad either thought my rides were an imposition or more likely that the walk home would discourage me from going in the first place. Neither changed my routine.

After getting off the train I would walk about a mile through the residential part of town and from then on it was pretty much open country. During the last hour of my walk, it was then long after midnight, I would encounter only three or four cars during the entire time. Today (2013) Dundee Road is a four lane highway with traffic twenty four hours a day.

About three quarters of a mile from home I would pass Sky Harbor Airport on my right and a small cemetery on the left. I was always much more comfortable if I could have a car passing me from either front or back as I hurriedly walked past that cemetery. My boyhood schoolmate, Charles Palmer, the boy who had drowned one summer in the dirty Des Plaines River was buried there. However, his grave was not the reason for my nervousness. I just didn't like the cemetery at night, any cemetery.

None of these inconveniences, the train ride to and from her house, the walk through the park or the long walk home in the dark could keep me from Eleanora's side whenever I had the chance to be with her. I was smitten.

Later that spring and summer, when I had access to my brother Elmer's Model A Ford, Eleanora and I would spend warm happy evenings together in the Forest Preserve's "lover's lane". We became very intimate but never want "all the way" as was the common expression in those days.

In early August Eleanora left on a train trip vacation to visit friends in New Mexico and her cousin Ted Czieslak in Seattle, Washington. The day she left I went to see her at the train station. She had already boarded the train so I went her car where my appearance was totally unexpected, and her question was. "Does you mother know you're here?" I was surprised but realized her question was a pretty good example of her opinion of my family home life at that time.

After Eleanora left on her trip my life on the peony farm became more and more unpleasant. My jobs at the time were very distasteful to me. I did not like picking the beans and other vegetables my father grew to supplement the family diet. I did this work along with Ed "Doc" Hunsaker who my father employed at the time. I was thoroughly unhappy and restless. So after Eleanora had been gone a short time, and although she was scheduled to return home in about two weeks, I decided one day to follow her out west.

XXVIII

Before daylight on the morning of Wednesday, August 20th, I left a note for my parents and started hitch-hiking west. I had a bankroll of exactly $8. I walked the first mile down Dundee Road west to Wheeling and started trying to thumb a ride. I made a mistake initially by not realizing I should take US Highway 30 going west. I picked up a ride going north on Milwaukee Avenue after which I started serious hitch hiking west on Highway 20. After a few false starts with short rides, a middle aged couple in a 1937 Dodge took me as far as Fort Dodge, Iowa.

My first night out was spent sleeping in the city park. It was a warm evening and I was not uncomfortable lying on the grass. Before turning in for the night I strolled into a very small hamburger stand. Just after I sat down a fast moving car came squealing up in front of the place. The driver slammed on the brakes and a young man rushed in and threatened the clerk behind the counter. He claimed the clerk had stolen some shoes of his and he appeared ready to fight with him. I don't know the outcome because I left hurriedly and when I looked back from across the street it seemed as though no serious trouble had actually occurred.

Next morning, since Highway 20 was not my best bet to get out west, I hitched a ride a short five or so miles south of Fort Dodge to Highway 30, named the Lincoln Highway. This major US highway ran from the east coast to its termination in the San Francisco area.

While standing along Route 30 trying to hitch a ride I noticed three or four round corn cribs in the field across the road. In the 1960s I drove several times between Salt Lake City and Chicago on Interstate 80 which parallels old Route 30. Although more than 30 years had passed since I originally stood beside those corn cribs I would occasionally divert from the Interstate so I could pass by them. At first I didn't expect to see them still there. But they were and may be there yet for all I know.

After a couple short rides on US 30 I was picked up near Missouri Valley, Iowa by a man driving a brand new 1942 Ford. In those days it was customary to drive a new car about 35 miles an hour for a few miles to "break in" the engine, so it was pretty slow going. But I was on my way.

Cars in those days had no air conditioning so we would drive for awhile with the hot wind in our faces. But it soon became extremely uncomfortable with all that hot air. Then we would close the windows. But the relief of the wind out of our faces felt good only until the air became stifling once more and we opened the windows again. This went on all day, so after a very long and very hot day of driving I got as far as North Platte, Nebraska and spent the night there.

Driving through Wyoming the next day was much cooler, although we still continued on at the slow 35mph pace. The man produced a bottle of whisky and offered me a drink which I took. Soon I could feel the effects of the booze and the trip became more pleasant.

By now I had already nearly run out money and so was unable to pay the necessary 50 cents for a hotel room in Evanston, Wyoming that Friday night. But I booked a room anyway and skipped out on the bill next day.

That night in the hotel bar I got my first look at the "Wild West". The place was full of rough looking hombres, very boisterous, and I thought it best not to hang around too long. As a young man I was quite inexperienced with people like the ones I encountered in Wyoming that night. I little knew, of course, what an important part Wyoming, as well as Utah, would play in my life some day, starting at the time I met my future wife Jean in Rock Springs in 1945. Next day my ride informed me that he was going to Los Angeles and was turning south toward Provo, Utah and I got out of his car.

I was soon picked up by a strange young man who drove me into Salt Lake City. The fellow claimed to be an airline pilot but I doubted his story. On arriving in Salt Lake City the two of us stopped in a small café in 2nd East Street where he seemed to be known. At least he knew one of the waitresses to whom he said, "Irma, you've got a nice ass."

I spent the rest of that Saturday visiting the Mormon Temple Grounds. It was my first encounter with the Mormons. When the Temple Grounds Guide told me about Joseph Smith and the story of the Angel Moroni I asked him what happened to the golden plates from which he claimed the Book of Mormon was translated. When he said an angel took them away I thought it was a wild story and wondered how anyone could believe it. Little did I know that some day I would be married to a Mormon woman and that the whole LDS way of life would have at least some affect on me. But that was far in advance of this summer day in 1941.

About 5 in the afternoon I again continued my peregrination west by hitch hiking north toward Ogden, Utah . A man who said he was going to Oregon gave me a ride to Boise, Idaho. But first we stopped in Ogden, where he spent a short time in one of the local brothels on 25th Street while I waited in the lobby.

We drove most of the way through Idaho after dark. About midnight we passed through the little town of Glenn's Ferry. It was quite late when the young man and I arrived in Boise where we shared a room in a cheap hotel. I was supposed to pay for half the cost of the room but I had little money and early the next day I left the hotel before daylight. Boise is another city that would mean much to my life many years later, but some experiences were not very pleasant.

I walked to the edge of town where I picked up a ride, but only to Nampa some 40 miles west. I had a lot of nerve because this was undoubtedly the highway my left-behind-friend would also be taking to Oregon. He would have seen me except that by luck Sunday morning the Nampa streets were deserted. So I could have seen him coming and ducked behind a tree until he passed. On the road one has to consider all the options.

As I stood waiting for a ride an old model T Ford came chugging down the highway. Although the place where I stood was still in town the street was 4 lanes wide. The Model T stopped just short of where I stood. A very old man got out of the car and I was surprised to see that early in the morning he was drunk and staggering. Just then a young boy about ten or twelve came out of the house where the old man had stopped. The old man fell to the ground in front of the car whose engine had died in the meantime. The kid took a quick look at the old duffer and said, "Oh grandpa, are you drunk again?" I soon got another ride out of Nampa and left that little drama to unfold.

My ride took me only a couple hundred miles to Baker, Oregon. In 1941 Baker was very small and it took me only a few minutes to walk to the western side of town which actually put me out in open country.

On this August Sunday mrning the narrow two lane road was deserted in both directions. On either side, broken down rusted barbed wire fences guarded desolate fields of what remained of the last harvest. It had obviously been a poor crop of wheat or barley. The fence was made of two stands of twisted barbed wire held up by old dried-out fence posts made of split logs. The sparse stubble in the fields stretched out and dissolved into the horizon.

To my right, the road was lined with grey split telephone poles with three or four wires on cross bars with their green connectors bright in the blazing sun. I was tired, clad in wrinkled clothes, and no doubt appeared as abandoned myself as the narrow shimmering road baking in the merciless Oregon sun. The absolute silence was stunning. Not the sound of a bird or even the wind. Probably no person anywhere ever felt as alone as I did that day. But in my unsophisticated youth I had no feeling of fear about being completely isolated, waiting to get a ride out of that barren landscape.

I was almost 20 years old but couldn't have been more naive. I was taking this long lone journey assuming Eleanora's cousin at the other end would welcome me. It never occurred to me that they might not want me there, or may not have room for me. I had grown up in the security of a stable home with friends and neighbors I could depend on. As I stood along the Oregon road I knew only that I needed a ride. After several frustrating hours in the blazing sun, an old car finally stopped and gave me a lift.

The drive along the Columbia River was the first time I had seen that enormous western river and I was amazed to see such sparse vegetation along its banks, especially across the river in Washington State. In August the hills are of a varied tan, yellow and beige hue and to me the rolling hills appeared magnificent beneath the blistering sun.

My ride let out in Le Grande, Oregon. It was near nightfall and I was tired and hungry. I was now in northeastern Oregon. LeGrande is a small town of about ten thousand people. The road, still US 30, I had been traveling on all day had been ascending, so now I was in rather high country. Because LeGrande is in a mountainous area I could tell it was going to get cold at night.

I walked and looked around town where I ran into some fellows who suggested that we all go down to the railroad yard and hop a freight train. I declined to go. I was afraid they would have robbed me of what little I had. That was the Bolivia watch my parents had given me when I graduated from High School, plus three dollars from my original eight.

When it got really dark and quite chilly I walked into the small residential part of town and there I crawled onto the back seat of someone's parked car where I spent the night. When I awoke next morning it was already daylight and I could hear people talking on the porch across the street from the car. I quietly opened the door on the side opposite the voices and slowly slid out onto the ground. After crawling far enough so the voices became fainter I got up and walked into town. I was now pretty stiff and hungry but at least had had a fairly good night's sleep.

I went out on the highway and tried to hitch a ride. After awhile a man in a Lincoln Zephyr coupe showed down and I thought I had a ride. I began trotting toward the car but it sped away. Although I was disappointed I soon got another ride as far as Arlington, Oregon.

At that point the road along the Oregon bank of the Columbia River ran along a ridge parallel to the river. As we approached Arlington the road turned slightly to the right toward the river, then ran down a rather steep incline and made a left turn into town.. As we made the turn toward the river we looked to our left and saw the Lincoln upside down on a street below. The driver had failed to negotiate the turn and had rolled down the hill. I felt I was very lucky the driver had ignored me.

Arlington was as far as my ride took me but I never went over to the turned-over car to see if anyone was injured. I was too intent on getting another lift. It was now noon and I was very hungry. I tried to pawn my high school watch at a gas station. The station owner refused and showed me the back of one of his station doors where I saw ten or fifteen other watches he had accepted for money to get some poor traveler out of town.

On the road across from the station I met a young man who was also looking for a lift. After listening to the story of my plight, he said he had a job and gave me six silver dollars with the provision I would return the money by helping some other poor unfortunate in the future. Over the years since that lucky day, I have paid the money back many times to other travelers.

I was unable to get a ride all that afternoon. But finally about five o'clock an older man, wife and granddaughter in a very rickety car picked me up. It was very slow going in their old car and daylight was running out. But finally we got to Klamath Falls where they let me out of the car.

I used part of the money the young man had given me to get a cheap hamburger and to buy a bus ticket to Portland. In Portland I noticed the bus station was close to the Portland Art Museum, so I walked over and slept that night on the grass behind a small wall in front of the Museum.

Next day, almost broke again, I hitched a ride as far as the Boeing Aircraft plant in Seattle. From there I walked all the rest of the day, over 20 miles, to get to Eleanora's cousin's house in the 4600 North block. On the way I found 10 pennies on a bridge over which I learned later was Union Lake.

I got to Czieslak's home about sundown and I was dead tired. Eleanora, although quite astonished, didn't really act surprised and quickly introduced me to her relatives. I immediately went to bed, slept all night and almost the entire next day. I came out and sat with them on their porch about sunset.

I had no idea, or cared at the time, what the Czieslaks thought of me. In my unsophisticated ignorance it didn't even occur to me what a lot of gall I had busting in uninvited on people who didn't know me and probably had never even heard of me. I had no way of notifying Eleanora that I was coming. A costly phone call was out of the question. But she was very happy to see me and didn't ask me to explain why I had made such a foolish trip. Maybe she wasn't as sophisticated as I thought.

Since I was completely broke, Eleanora borrowed ten bucks from her cousin's wife Harriet and we went to the movies. This turned out to be our only night out together. We began a very short romantic period in Czieslak's home when we were alone. We became very intimate and talked seriously about marriage.

On Labor Day the Czieslaks took Eleanora and me, with their girls, for a drive part way up Mount Rainer. The Czieslaks had two girls, Judith about 12 and the other, a nasty little brat about 6. We took some pictures with a Kodak Brownie camera and had tiny black and white pictures printed. I still have a couple of the pictures. Everything seemed to be going very well between us and I felt pretty good.

Eleanora and I talked about staying in Seattle and she considered applying for a teaching job there. But time was short and not enough left, so she took the train back to Chicago and her job at Grove School.

Immediately after Eleanora left for home Mrs. Czieslak tried to get me to go to Canada and join the Canadian Air Force which was already engaged in the war in Europe.

I declined and left Czieslaks and stayed a few days in St. Vincent DePaul's homeless shelter. My meals were made up of wretchedly foul food with moldy Twinkies for desert. Later Ted Czieslak found me employment at a company called Trumbull Electric. My job was to assemble electrical panel parts and the pay was minimal. I worked in a dingy, poorly lit factory, taking the 7AM bus to work in pouring rain darkness.

I wrote to Eleanora and she wrote back but I could tell from her letters she was getting tired of my juvenile behavior. I spent my free time in Seattle walking around downtown. It was near Christmas now and I was fascinated by the colorful displays and animated figures in the big store windows. I began to dislike Seattle but never admitted to myself why I had been stupid enough to come there in the first place.

On Sunday, December 7th, I spent part of a rare sunny afternoon looking at the animals in the Woodland Park Zoo. When I came home I heard the news about the sneak attack on Pearl Harbor.

That attack turned out to be the end of the Great Depression. People went back to work, mainly in war industries, and some, both men and women, went into military service. I spent two years in the Naval Air Corps.

I wrote Eleanora several more times during my time at the factory but our relationship deteriorated even more from then on. I suppose Harriet also wrote her and enumerated the sordid details of my stay with the Czieslaks and about my job at the electric manufacturing company.

Eventually I saved enough from my meager pay for a ticket to Chicago and home. Upon boarding the slow Milwaukee RR train my Seattle adventure was over. I never saw the Czieslaks again.

Eleanora had told me more than once that one of her major goals in life was to marry a doctor. She didn't know any doctors. But her youngest sister Gloria was dating a medical student so Eleanora married him. She told me her sister was very unhappy about the marriage and I suppose Gloria had good reason. Eleanora and Gloria looked very much alike.

After a long train trip, the train being help up a long time in Montana because of an accident, I arrived home shortly before Christmas. While still in the Chicago Union Station I met former school mate Edwin Henning who told me of Billy Christman's death in a car crash. Billy was gone and so was the dream of H&C Movie Company.

I saw Eleanora just a few times after returning. Once at her house when the family had a memorial for her brother who had died in the service. Another time we met by chance after she had married the doctor and she had her little girl with her. Our relationship was long over by then.

One other time I had seen her on a double deck bus in Chicago. I was sitting way in the back and she and a man were far in the front of the bus and didn't see me. I guessed the man was her sister's boy friend.

In 1992 when I was looking in a phone book for the number of some friends in Pleasanton, California I suddenly came across the name Edward Schlies, MD. I knew that was the name of the man she had married. So I called the number and explained who I was and Eleanora came on the phone. We talked a long time about the past and caught up on each other's news.

Since I was nearby in Southern California, we immediately agreed to meet once again. We wrote and exchanged pictures but never got together. By then the six year difference in age had begun to show. She had changed so much in appearance I hardly recognized her in the pictures she sent. She had been so pretty.

With the Japanese attack the country went to war and The Great Depression was at an end. Life in America, and for me, would never be the same. A door had closed and another had opened. The country started a New Era and I began a New Life.

Epilog.

If there was one word to describe the 1930s that word would be Stability. Times may have been tough in the 30s but they stayed pretty much the same all through the Great Depression. If there is a word to describe conditions today I think the word would be Undependable. No one can depend on tomorrow being anything like today. And too much of the time "tomorrow" is a disappointment to many people.

I would not trade my life during the Great Depression for any other time that came after, or before. Only we who lived through it all can truly know what America was like in the

1930s. Even with the many problems the country faced, The United States was truly united then. We were folks who stuck it out together. It was a time of social amity that is gone forever.

While living through the 13 years of the Great Depression my brothers and I were fortunate to live in a home that was one of stability, with responsible parents who always provided us with security and what comfort they could. There were many reasons for our feeling of security, but by far the most important was because our mother and father were always there and could be depended on. They provided stability in our home life as well as guidance and punishment when it was needed.

Our father was a truly self-made successful man, although I know he had ups and downs too. My brothers and I never realized until many years later what building and operating the peony farm meant to my mother and dad. Dad's example was a great influence on me and my becoming independent and always having that strong desire to own my own business like he did.

When I am asked today what life was like during the Great Depression I can assure them the times were far different from the depression that started about 2008.

During the 1930s there was a feeling of togetherness in the neighborhoods of Chicago and suburbs. No one locked their doors at night. The back door of our home was never locked.

The 1930 censes showed that the entire population of the United States was 123,202,624 million men, women and children. I don't remember if they listed by race.

Most of the people in America had come from various parts of Europe, or were descendants of those who had come from there. The feeling in the country was that we were all part of one big family. I guess it was a European family, transplanted to the USA. We were in trouble in the 1930s, but we were all in the "same boat".

That feeling continued into and through the Second World War, with scrap drives, bond sales and the Hollywood Canteen. But the oneness gradually disappeared with the end of the War.

In 1945 the terrible war had been won. The Great Depression was over and a new era was beginning.

After my service in the Navy I went home in 1945 to a succession of jobs in Chicago Commercial Art Studios where I had the good fortunate to work with some of the greatest artists in the country. I also worked as a copywriter before starting my own shop in Salt Lake City in 1960.

My life in the ad agency I had during the 1960s, 70s and 80s was far different than the Depression life I enjoyed in the 1930s.

By 1965 the whole country had turned upside down but we people from the 30s adjusted easily to the new way of life. Living through the Great Depression had given us a definite advantage over everyone else. I am thankful for those years, the life we lived and advantages it gave us..

In September, 1945 I had met Jean Daniels in Rock Springs, Wyoming. We corresponded, spent much time on the telephone, dated and were married in Chicago in 1947. We had two daughters, Anita and Rhonda.

Jean passed away at the young age of 71. Both daughters, Anita and Rhonda, have passed on too. I miss them all. Jean and I had nearly 37 wonderful years of married life together.